Bloom's

GUIDES

Arthur Miller's
The Crucible

1984
All the Pretty Horses
Beloved
Brave New World
The Crucible
Cry, the Beloved Country
Death of a Salesman
Hamlet
The Handmaid's Tale
The House on Mango Street
I Know Why the Caged Bird Sings
Lord of the Flies
Macbeth
Maggie: A Girl of the Streets
Ragtime
The Scarlet Letter
Snow Falling on Cedars
To Kill a Mockingbird

Bloom's
GUIDES

Arthur Miller's
The Crucible

Edited & with an Introduction
by Harold Bloom

CHELSEA HOUSE
PUBLISHERS
A Haights Cross Communications Company
Philadelphia

First Printing
1 3 5 7 9 8 6 4 2

Library of Congress Cataloging-in-Publication Data

Arthur Miller's The crucible / edited and with an introduction by Harold Bloom.
        p. cm. — (Bloom's guides)
    Includes bibliographical references and index.
    ISBN 0-7910-7876-0
    1. Miller, Arthur, 1915- Crucible. 2. Trials (Witchcraft) in literature. 3. Salem (Mass.)—In literature. 4. Witchcraft in literature. [1. Miller, Arthur, 1915- Crucible. 2. American literature—History and criticism.] I. Title: Crucible. II. Bloom, Harold. III. Series.
    PS3525.I5156C7337 2004
    812'.52—dc22
                                                2003025728

Chelsea House Publishers
1974 Sproul Road, Suite 400
Broomall, PA 19008-0914

www.chelseahouse.com

Contributing editor: Pamela Loos
Cover design by Takeshi Takahashi
Layout by EJB Publishing Services

Contents

Introduction

HAROLD BLOOM

Nearly fifty years ago, in his introduction to his *Collected Plays*, Arthur Miller meditated upon *The Crucible*, staged four years before, in 1953. A year after that first production, Miller was refused a passport, and in 1956–57 he endured the active persecution of the American witch-hunt for suspected Communists. The terror created in some of his former friends and associates by the possibility of being branded as warlocks and witches "underlies every word in *The Crucible*," according to Miller. "Every word" necessarily is hyperbolical, since *The Crucible* attempts to be a personal tragedy as well as a social drama. Miller, Ibsen's disciple, nevertheless suffers an anxiety of influence in *The Crucible* not so much in regard to Ibsen's *An Enemy of the People* but in relation to George Bernard Shaw's *Saint Joan*. The frequent echoes of *Saint Joan* seem involuntary, and are distracting, and perhaps fatal to the aesthetic value of *The Crucible*. For all its moral earnestness, *Saint Joan* is enhanced by the Shawian ironic wit, a literary quality totally absent from Miller, here and elsewhere. Though a very well-made play, *The Crucible* rarely escapes a certain dreariness in performance, and does not gain by rereading.

This is not to deny the humane purpose nor the theatrical effectiveness of *The Crucible*, but only to indicate a general limitation, here and elsewhere, in Miller's dramatic art. Eric Bentley has argued shrewdly that "one never knows what a Miller play is about: politics or sex." Is *The Crucible* a personal tragedy, founded upon Proctor's sexual infidelity, or is it a play of social protest and warning? There is no reason it should not be both, except for Miller's inability to fuse the genres. Here he falls short of his master, Ibsen, who concealed Shakespearean tragic purposes within frameworks of social issues, yet invariably unified the two modes. Still, one can be grateful that Miller has not revised *The Crucible* on the basis of his own afterthoughts, which have emphasized the absolute evil of the

Salem powers, Danforth and Hathorne. These worthies already are mere facades, opaque to Miller's understanding and our own. Whatever their religious sensibility may or may not have been, Miller has no imaginative understanding of it, and we therefore confront them only as puppets. Had Miller made them even more malevolent, our bafflement would have been even greater. I am aware that I tend to be an uncompromising aesthete, and I cannot dissent from the proven theatrical effectiveness of *The Crucible*. Its social benignity is also beyond my questioning; American society continues to benefit by this play. We would have to mature beyond our national tendency to moral and religious self-righteousness for *The Crucible* to dwindle into another period piece, and that maturation is nowhere in sight.

Biographical Sketch

Born in Manhattan on October 17, 1915, Arthur Miller was the second child of three for Isadore and Augusta Miller, a well-to-do Jewish couple. In 1929 the stock market crash and Depression forced Arthur Miller's father out of the coat business and their family out of their home to a small frame house in Brooklyn. Upon graduating from Abraham Lincoln High School in 1932, Miller started saving as much as he could from his income at an auto-parts warehouse so he could go to college. He occasionally would read on the subway on his way to work, and when he happened upon Dostoevsky's *The Brothers Karamazov*, Miller "all at once believed [he] was born to be a writer."

But when he applied to the University of Michigan, Miller was turned down until he tried for a third time with a convincing letter he sent to the admissions officer. Having heard the school gave writing prizes, he enrolled in journalism, and within eighteen months he began writing plays, winning the Avery Hopwood Award on his first try for a piece he had written in just four days, *Honors at Dawn*. He received another Hopwood for his second work, *No Villain*, just one year later in 1937.

After he received his B.A. in 1938, Miller went back to New York and worked with the Federal Theatre Project until it was abolished; he then found himself on welfare. He completed his play, *The Golden Years*, and to make money he wrote numerous radio scripts—work he hated. In 1940 Miller married Mary Grace Slattery, to whom he had become engaged at the University of Michigan; they moved to Brooklyn and eventually had two children. He held various odd jobs and kept writing for the next four years, while she served as the main breadwinner, working as a waitress and editor.

In 1944, Miller had his first Broadway production. The play's title, *The Man Who Had All the Luck*, certainly wasn't applicable to Miller at the time, for the piece struggled through only six performances, although it managed to win the Theatre Guild National Award. A back injury kept Miller out of the military, but he visited army camps during the war and published his journal, *Situation Normal*, in 1944. By 1945 Miller switched gears and wrote a novel, *Focus*, about anti-Semitism. He became increasingly involved in leftist organizations and liberal causes. Then in 1947 his first son was born, and his first successful Broadway play was produced, *All My Sons*. It showed the after-effects of World War II on a family whose father had sold faulty plane parts to the government.

But Miller's most famous play by far became *Death of a Salesman*, which centered on a dejected salesman's final days. It was composed in six weeks on a typewriter Miller had bought with the money he earned from his first Hopwood. That year—1949—the Pulitzer Prize was awarded for the first time—to Miller. He also received the New York Drama Critics' Circle Award for the work, which continued through 1950 for 742 performances. The same year Miller traveled to California to work on a film project. There he met Marilyn Monroe and they saw each other frequently for many weeks.

In 1951 Miller published an adaptation of Henrik Ibsen's *An Enemy of the People*. Political commitments took up much of Miller's time then, and in 1953 he put his warnings about the dangers of mass hysteria and government power into the form of *The Crucible*, a work about the Salem witch trials that was readily construed as a metaphor for the McCarthy hearings then taking place. By 1955 Miller's marriage was falling apart, and he met Monroe again at a theater party. They were seen together more often, and after his divorce, Miller married Marilyn Monroe in 1956.

The Crucible was well-received, but it helped bring Miller negative attention of another sort. In June of 1956 he was subpoenaed to come before the House Un-American Activities Committee. Curiously, in the midst of his political troubles, he announced that he and Monroe had been secretly married. Before the Committee, Miller freely admitted his past associations with leftist groups, stating they had ended in 1950. Refusing to be a "good citizen" who would identify other Communists, he named not one.

During this time, in 1955, Miller saw his *A View from the Bridge* produced on a double bill with a short play, *A Memory of Two Mondays*. He also won his second Pulitzer Prize. His screenplay for the 1961 film *The Misfits* was created for his wife, who starred in it with Clark Gable, but shortly thereafter in that same year, they were divorced. Also in that year, Miller's mother died at the age of eighty.

In 1962, Miller married the photographer Inge Morath, with whom he had two children and collaborated on several books, writing text to accompany her images. By 1964, Miller's *After the Fall* was produced, creating more controversy than any of his previous work. Many critics balked at what they construed to be an excessively autobiographical piece.

Miller covered the Nazi trials in Frankfurt for the *New York Herald Tribune* and then wrote *Incident at Vichy* (1965), a short play about Nazism and anti-Semitism in Vichy France. In the same year he traveled extensively in Europe to oversee productions of his various works.

In 1966 approximately seventeen million viewers saw *Death of a Salesman* on television, twenty times the number who had seen the play when it was on Broadway. A collection of short stories, *I Don't Need You Anymore* (1967) followed, as did another play, *The Price* (1968). He was a member of the Connecticut delegation to the fateful Democratic National Convention in 1972, and he continued to be politically active and speak out for his beliefs. In 1973 the comic *The Creation of the World and Other Business* was produced, and later the *The Archbishop's Ceiling* (1977) and *The American Clock* (1980).

In 1983 Miller directed *Death of a Salesman* in China. In 1984 *Up from Paradise* was published, followed by *Danger: Memory!* in 1986, and his autobiography, *Timebends: A Life*, in 1987. He continued to see his works published and produced not only in theater but also on television. In 1994 *Broken Glass* was published, and in 1995 production began on a film version of *The Crucible*. A collection of his essays was published in 2000, and in 2002 his play *Resurrection Blues* was produced.

Miller continues to write in his Connecticut home. Dustin Hoffman, one of the most famous Willy Lomans, describes

Miller in *Arthur Miller and Company* as "so articulate. He's this great storyteller. He sounds like this New York cab driver; he's so unpretentious and earthy. You're laughing one minute, then you're thinking the next, and touched the next."

The Story Behind the Story

When *The Crucible* was published and produced in 1953, many audiences and critics felt that the play, with a plot focused on the Salem witch trials of the late 1600s, was an analogy for the McCarthy investigations that were going on at the time. Some of the same issues, such as mass hysteria and unchecked power were at the forefront of both historical events.

In the 1950s, the U.S. House of Representatives' Un-American Activities Committee questioned people that were suspected of being Communists. The Committee interviewed individuals about their activities and also asked them for names of other suspected Communists. Many were blacklisted, fired from their jobs, and would not be hired elsewhere. Miller cites the extreme case of a man who was fired because he explained that he had no connections with leftists and had nothing he could give the court, namely a confession; as a result of the trauma, the man could not summon the strength to leave his home for more than a year. Miller himself was subpoenaed a few years after *The Crucible* was produced and testified that his associations with leftist groups had ended in 1950. He would not supply names of others he knew to have such associations at that time or in the past, voicing his belief against such an action in nearly the same words used by a character in his own play.

The events of the 1950s disturbed Miller, as he would later describe in his introduction to his *Collected Plays*, which was published in 1957:

> It was not only the rise of "McCarthyism" that moved me, but something which seemed much more weird and mysterious. It was the fact that a political, objective, knowledgeable campaign from the far Right was capable of creating not only a terror, but a new subjective reality....The wonder of it all struck me that so practical and picayune a cause, carried forward by such manifestly ridiculous men, should be capable of paralyzing thought

itself, and worse, causing to billow up such persuasive clouds of "mysterious" feelings within people....

With this in mind, Miller turned to the Salem witch trials, events he had similarly thought were nearly incomprehensible. He did extensive research on these trials using, among other things, various public records in Salem. Miller realized this was the right venue for his new play when he discovered one piece of information, namely that Abigail, the leader of the hysterical girls who appeared in court, had accused Elizabeth Proctor of being a witch but had not accused Elizabeth's husband, John. Miller changed historical events here slightly when he wrote his play, in that he raised Abigail's age and lowered John Proctor's to make an affair between them believable. He created the affair as Abigail's prime motivator for accusing Elizabeth. Even though there was no historical record of it, Miller felt it appropriate based on information he read. Some critics have called the affair forced; others have seen it as a device that works.

Other such reasons also have been known to prompt the people in Salem at the time to accuse fellow citizens of witchcraft. For example, victims of societal prejudice were accused first—a black slave from a far-away land and another woman who was poverty-stricken and pregnant but unmarried. Similarly, prior to the trials, men were frequently creating reasons for suing landowners out of jealously because of their better animals and/or land. Once the witch trials began, Thomas Putnam, it was said, told his daughter who to accuse in court, knowing that he would be able to purchase the convicted man's property while he was serving his sentence in prison. Another reason for an accusation was explained to Miller after *The Crucible* was produced. In a letter from a descendent of John Proctor, it was cited that Proctor was an amateur inventor of items that others found suspicious because of their ingenuity.

Some critics have accused Miller of inaccuracies in his portrayal of the Salem circumstances, and numerous essays have been written—both pro and con—on this topic. In the printed play, Miller includes a note just prior to its beginning explaining that his goal was not to recreate an exact history, and he enumerates the changes he has made and why.

Over time, *The Crucible* has become Miller's most frequently produced play. Some critics see this as proof that the play is not just about the witch trials or McCarthyism but is universal. This, in fact, was Miller's goal, as he described it: "I wished for a way to write a play that would be sharp, that would lift out of the morass of subjectivism the squirming, single, defined process which would show that the sin of public terror is that it divests man of conscience, of himself."

Miller has written extensively on theater, and in a piece for the *New York Times* after *The Crucible* was completed but before it was produced, he voiced a similar viewpoint to the one above, although in a different context. In the piece, he writes about the state of theater but makes no mention of *The Crucible*. He compares a negative force at work in the movie industry to one similar but less influential in theater, namely a practical, financial force to keep movies within certain boundaries and therefore similar and no longer risky. Miller describes it:

> But we [in the theater] have an atmosphere of dread just the same, an unconsciously—or consciously—accepted party line, a sanctified complex of moods and attitudes, proper and improper. If nothing else comes of it, one thing surely has: it has made it dangerous to dare, and, worse still, impractical. I am not speaking merely of political thought. Journalists have recently made studies of college students now in school and have been struck by the absence among them of any ferment, either religious, political, literary, or whatever. Wealthy, powerful, envied all about, it seems the American people stand mute.

List of Characters

Reverend Samuel Parris is a widower in his mid-forties who seems more concerned about his reputation as town minister than he is about his parishioners or his troubled daughter. He is repressive, insecure, vain, and paranoid, openly showing the worst qualities of the worst of the town's inhabitants. While he is quick to caution the townspeople against seeing his daughter as a witch, he is just as quick to support the authorities in condemning so many others once the witch trials commence.

Betty Parris is the minister's ten-year-old daughter, who has been caught dancing in the woods. Guilt ridden and fearful of what may happen to her, she accuses others of being witches to cast blame elsewhere.

Tituba, a native of Barbados, is the slave in the Parris household and in her forties. She functions as an example of the downtrodden who is an easy target; looked down upon for being black, she is blamed for Betty Parris's "illness" and is the first to be accused of witchcraft when the suspicious townspeople notice things happening that are unexplainable.

Abigail Williams is Parris's beautiful seventeen-year-old orphaned niece who lives with his family. She was previously employed by the Proctors, and while there she tempted John Proctor. Powerful, manipulative, and evil, she sees goodness as a sham, needs to cover her mistakes, and is willing to commit murder to get what she wants. She leads the girls in their accusations in court against some of the most well-respected and good townspeople.

Mrs. Ann Putnam, wife of Thomas, is described as "a twisted soul of forty-five." Seven of her children have died as babies, and since she cannot understand a reason for their deaths and is superstitious, she believes a murdering witch is responsible.

Thomas Putnam is nearly fifty, the oldest son of the town's richest man, and most vindictive. He is a prime example of the evil in the village, believing himself superior to most and looking for revenge for past grievances. He has attempted to use force to get his way in the past but has always failed. Deeply embittered, he accuses many of being witches, frequently is a witness against those accused, and has a daughter who at times leads the hysterical girls in the finger-pointing.

Mary Warren is the Proctor family's weak and impressionable seventeen-year-old servant. Initially awed by Abigail's strength, she later summons the courage to call the girls frauds in court but then again succumbs to their evil pressures.

John Proctor is an independent-minded, well-respected, strong Salem farmer in his mid-thirties and the main protagonist. He is plagued with guilt over a secret. Alternately labeled "very human" or "too good" by drama critics, no one denies he is transformed as the play progresses.

Rebecca Nurse is the ultimate good, religious community member. She takes on a near God-like aura when she first appears on stage and quiets a troubled child merely by her loving, calm presence.

Francis Nurse is the highly regarded resident of Salem who organizes a petition in support of his accused wife.

Giles Corey is in his early eighties, "a crank and a nuisance" who is constantly blamed for numerous things that go wrong in the town but is not guilty. Corey is independent and brave, someone who can reinforce the beliefs of Proctor yet who cannot serve as too strong of an aid because of his foibles.

Reverend John Hale, almost forty, is from a nearby town and is the recognized authority on witchcraft. He depends on information from books that he believes hold all the answers.

Initially he is intent on doing good but does not realize the trouble he has helped create. He is one of the more developed characters that experiences a change but becomes enlightened too late.

Elizabeth Proctor is first presented as the aggrieved wife of John and later as loving and understanding. Throughout the play, the community views her as one of its upright members, but she is more complex than a stereotype of goodness. She recognizes her faults and asks her husband for forgiveness, seeing herself as contributing to his own sin.

Ezekiel Cheever is a marshall of the court whose unquestioned obedience to authority leads him to gather "evidence" for the trial and comply with every order.

Judge Hathorne is one of the judges sent to question the accused witches. He is in his sixties, bitter, remorseless and the foil for Proctor and the upright citizens. He is concerned more about his power than true justice, charging those who bring new evidence to court as being in contempt. In hindsight, Miller said he would have made this character even more evil.

Deputy Governor Danforth is the judge overseeing the witch trials in the highest court of the government of the province. In his sixties, grave and intent on upholding the power of the state at all costs, he is intelligent and at times open-minded but seduced by the girls' demonstration in court. In describing his court and how questioning proceeds, he says, "We burn a hot fire here."

Marshall Herrick is a man in his early thirties who works for the court yet feels some sympathy for those accused.

Summary and Analysis

While throughout the play there are several notes from Miller, usually providing background on characters, the longest of these occurs at the opening to **Act 1**. Here, however, the focus is on the community and its history, rather than the characters in the play. We are taken to the spring of 1692 in Salem, Massachusetts, a time of great austerity and discipline, when undying work was required just to cultivate the land and make a living in this still-new world. The Puritan parents of these settlers had been persecuted in England, and, ironically, these descendants now rejected other religions as well, to keep their ways preserved from "wrong ways and deceitful ideas."

For these people, there was a great value in community, since there was still an element of danger in this land that was on the edge of unconquered wilderness. Yet at the same time the danger was starting to lessen and, as a result, some of the rules were disturbing to those more independent-minded inhabitants such as the main character of the play. A questioning of the usual systems and pressure for signs of greater individual freedom were what caused unease among many. This set the stage for the witch hunts, which, in an area where nearly all inhabitants knew the business of everyone else, also provided a most perverse outlet for expressing long-standing hatred of certain neighbors as well as jealousy against those with good or extensive land and livestock.

The **first scene** in Act I opens in a bedroom in Reverend Samuel Parris's house, where Parris's daughter Betty is lying in bed completely still and he is kneeling next to her, praying and crying. He is interrupted by his slave Tituba, whose only concern seems to be for Betty's welfare, yet Parris drives her out of the room. Next his niece Abigail enters and then Susanna Walcott, who brings a message from the doctor that he cannot find a remedy for Betty and believes her illness may have been brought on by "unnatural causes," that is, witchcraft. Parris looks at Susanna wide-eyed and tells her that this is not so and that he has sent for Reverend Hale to confirm it. He asks that she tell the doctor to keep consulting his books for a treatment.

When Susanna leaves, Abigail tells her uncle that many of the townspeople have heard about Betty's plight and the witchcraft rumor and a crowd has gathered in the parlor, waiting for an explanation. Now he presses Abigail, and we learn of the events that precipitated Betty's illness. Parris insists that Abigail tell him the truth before his enemies, who want to remove him as minister, learn it on their own. Parris tells her he saw the girls dancing in the "heathen" woods. Abigail swears they were only dancing and nothing else happened in the woods. He then tells her he saw Tituba waving her arms over the fire and screeching gibberish, to which Abigail explains that she was just singing her usual Barbados songs. Parris adds that he saw a dress on the ground and perhaps someone running naked, at which point the teenager is terrified and denies that anyone was naked.

Parris then turns to another issue and asks his niece if there is any blemish on her own reputation, to which she responds that there is none. He has heard people say that Goody Proctor, who discharged Abigail from employment in the Proctor home, has hardly attended church, to avoid being near Abigail, whom she describes as "something soiled." Abigail explains that Goody hates her because Abigail would not be her slave and that Goody is a bitter, horrible woman. But Parris notes that no one else has tried to hire Abigail in the seven months since she was dismissed. At this point, Abigail's temper shows as she denies the charge again and again calls Goody a liar. The scene between Abigail and her uncle is reminiscent of a courtroom scene and certainly provokes some of the tension we imagine will arise later in the play. Also, the scene reveals Parris's suspicion of Abigail, even though he is her uncle; this coupled with her behavior makes the reader suspicious of her as well. Similarly, we become uneasy at the range of her responses, which change from somewhat deferential to quick-tempered.

The questioning is interrupted when Mrs. Ann Putnam enters and shortly thereafter her husband, Thomas Putnam. Both of the Putnams believe witchcraft is at work, although

Parris vehemently denies it. The Putnams also say that their daughter is in a bad state, walking but unable to see, hear, or eat.

In the written play, Miller interrupts the action to provide background on Thomas Putnam, "a man with many grievances." Putnam is the oldest son of the richest man in town and believes himself superior to most. Among other things, he is still quite angry that the town turned against the candidate he had proposed for minister of Salem, his brother-in-law. Relying on his usual forcefulness, Putnam had also failed to change his father's will, which left more money to Putnam's stepbrother than to him. In reaction, Putnam accuses many of witchcraft once the panic sets in the town, is a witness against the accused in many of the trials, and has a daughter who provokes other girls to testify against the accused as well.

We return to the action as Mrs. Putnam, at her husband's prompting, explains to Parris that she has had seven babies die, and that Ruth, the only child still alive, had recently not been herself. To get to the bottom of the unusual circumstances, Mrs. Putnam sent Ruth to Tituba, so Tituba could connect her to speak with the dead children. Parris is astounded at the story, and reminds Mrs. Putnam that such an action is a "formidable sin," which lets the audience know that the Puritans have other superstitions as well as believing in witches. Mrs. Putnam believes Ruth did connect with her dead siblings.

Parris turns to Abigail and accuses her of conjuring spirits, but she says it was only Tituba and Ruth who were involved. Abigail hopes to absolve herself, but, of course, we realize that she is not guiltless, since she never told Parris this version when he had previously questioned her. Earlier Parris had reminded Abigail that he has taken her in and cared for her, and again he reminds her of how poorly she has repaid him.

Putnam makes the suggestion that Parris, now even more fearful, should admit what happened to the people gathered, rather than wait for their accusations against those in his house. Parris still believes he is doomed, but his exclamations are interrupted when the Putnams's servant, Mercy Lewis, enters and tells them that Ruth Putnam is a little better. Putnam again urges Parris to speak to the villagers downstairs, and finally Parris agrees only to pray with them but not to mention witchcraft.

Abigail is left in the room with only Mercy Lewis. Abigail, scared, goes to Betty and shakes her and yells at her, "Now stop this! Betty! Sit up now!" But Betty remains limp. Abigail tells Mercy that if she is questioned she should say that the girls were dancing in the woods. Mercy replies, "Aye. And what more?" Abigail adds that Parris also knows that Tituba was conjuring Ruth's sisters. Mercy again asks, "And what more?" Abigail tells her that Parris saw Mercy naked. Again, we see the lack of straightforwardness in Abigail. She only provides a piece of information with each "And what more?" that comes from Mercy. Also, we see Abigail lie when she is not even pressured, for Parris only said he saw a dress, but never said he saw Mercy naked.

Mary Warren enters breathless and asks the two girls what they should do now that the entire village believes there are witches about. Before waiting for their answers, Mary says they must tell what occurred, since witches are hanged and Abigail would only get whipped for the dancing. Abigail exclaims, "Oh, *we'll* be whipped!" But Mary quickly reminds her that she only watched the others. Mercy moves toward her threateningly, and then a sound is heard from Betty. Abigail goes over to her and asks her to wake up. She sits Betty up and shakes her violently, yelling "I'll beat you, Betty!" Again she lies, telling Betty that she has told Parris everything, in an attempt to keep the girl from fearing her fate.

But Betty jumps up and runs toward the window, saying she will fly to her dead mother. Abigail prevents Betty from jumping and again says that she has told Parris everything. But Betty is not so sickly as she seems, for she screams out that Abigail drank blood, a charm to kill John Proctor's wife, and that Abigail never told Parris this. With this, Abigail "smashes her across the face." Betty collapses into the bed, sobbing and crying for her mother. Abigail repeats to the girls what they are allowed to reveal—only that they danced and it was Tituba who did the conjuring. She warns the girls that she can seriously harm them, having seen Indians smash the heads of

22

her own parents. Mary Warren becomes frightened.

John Proctor enters the room. He is a farmer patience for hypocrites, is rather independent prime, confident, and strong. He yells for Mary to go home, and Mercy, too, is intimidated by him and leaves. Proctor goes to Betty, saying he has come to see what the town's uproar is about, and Abigail tells him just what she instructed the other girls to say about what happened. Abigail keeps moving closer to Proctor, telling him she's been waiting for him every night, to which he retorts that he has never given her justification for doing so. She reminds him of how he clutched her and says she knows he loved her then and still does, but he tells her she's speaking wildly, that he's hardly stepped off his farm for months. As she continues pushing him, he does admit that he has looked up at her bedroom window. With this, Abigail softens and starts to cry, then grabs him desperately again. When he gently pushes her away and starts to speak sympathetically, addressing her as "Child," she becomes quite angry.

John is pushed to anger, too, when Abigail starts to remark on the cruel coldness of his wife. Finally, he shakes her, and they hear the singing of a psalm from below, while Abigail, in tears, explains how she watches for the return of John Proctor, who enlightened her about the hypocrisy of the townspeople and their religion. So, theirs was not just a lustful relationship; Abigail believes he showed her the truth.

But as Proctor abruptly starts to leave, Betty suddenly covers her ears and moans loudly, causing her father to rush in, along with Mrs. Putnam, her husband, and Mercy. Rebecca Nurse enters, a woman of seventy-two who is highly respected in the community yet who also has enemies because her husband had earned a great amount of land, which provoked great fights with neighbors, one of whom was a Putnam. By this time, another older person has entered as well—Giles Corey, a strong eighty-three-year-old. All are quiet as Rebecca, exuding gentleness, nears Betty's bed. The girl calms down and is quiet as others in the room are astonished. Rebecca explains that she

...as numerous children and grandchildren of her own. She advises, "A child's spirit is like a child, you can never catch it by running after it; you must stand still, and, for love, it will soon itself come back." Proctor is the only one in the room who is in agreement with Rebecca; clearly these two already stand out from the other foolish and overly emotional characters.

As the scene unfolds, Proctor questions why Parris made the decision to send for Reverend Hale without consulting the villagers, to which Parris replies that he is sick of meetings. Mrs. Putnam again brings up all of the children she's lost, and now she can compare her tragedy to the smooth life of Rebecca, who has eleven children and twenty-six grandchildren. The comparisons and accusations grow here, with Mr. Putnam standing up for Parris. Putnam accuses Proctor of not being a good Christian, since he has not seen him at their Sabbath meetings for months, but Proctor explains that this is because Parris speaks only of damnation in his preachings and hardly ever of God.

Those in the room persist in arguing, with Proctor, Rebecca, and Corey usually voicing agreement against the others. Parris complains that he has not gotten the wood to keep himself warm, but the others explain that his salary includes extra money so he can buy wood. Proctor admonishes him for being the first minister ever to ask them for the deed to the meeting house, and finally, Parris, fed up, furiously tells him they are not Quakers and he should tell his followers so. At this Proctor asks who these followers are, and Putnam explains that there is a group against Parris and "all authority!" To this Proctor retorts that he, then, must go find the group, and all are shocked.

Rebecca tries to take the heat off Proctor by saying that he really did not mean what he said, but he counters, "I mean it solemnly, Rebecca; I like not the smell of this "'authority'." When Rebecca urges him to not "break charity" with Parris, he says he must go and get to work sowing and dragging home lumber, but even this simple comment can provide no easy escape, for Putnam accuses him of taking lumber from property that does not belong to him. Corey, who has just commented that there are too many fights and suings among the townspeople, says he too must go to work and tells Putnam they will win if Putnam dare fight them over the wood.

The bickering and reproach seem impossible to stop, and the Reverend Hale—the topic of the initial argument—enters the room. Again, Arthur Miller interrupts the written drama with a long description, this time providing some history of people's beliefs about the devil. For the Puritans, these beliefs also became entangled with politics, Miller explains. He also scoffs at the idea, which numerous critics have complained about, that the analogy between the fear of witches and fear of Communists is not valid, since witches could not exist but Communists do. But, Miller explains, he has no doubt that people in 1692 Salem *were* communing with, and even worshiping," the devil.

Hale is carrying a stack of heavy books, which he describes as needing to be heavy since "they are weighted with authority." The use of "authority," of course, draws us back to Proctor's use of it just shortly before, when he voiced his concern over Parris's seeming belief that one authority stands for all authority, which should never be questioned. Hale enters, then, reinforcing the belief that authority has weight and therefore validity; he does not question what these books contain.

The first person Hale recognizes is Rebecca Nurse, who he says he recognizes because of her reputation for goodness—she indeed looks like a good soul. This, of course, reinforces our view of her but does not say much for the other women in the room. Parris then introduces the Putnams, since he sees Putnam as an ally, and Hale exclaims over being in their "distinguished company." Hale immediately appears, then, not to favor one or the other of the camps that previously had shown themselves. John Proctor is cordial to Hale but slights the villagers and embarrasses Hale in the process, when he says since Hale is known to be a sensible man it would be beneficial to the town if he would leave some of that sensibility in Salem. With this, Proctor leaves, perhaps proving Corey's earlier statement that Proctor does not believe in witches, although Proctor had denied ever making such a statement.

The others left in the room immediately start to tell Hale of the unusual things they have seen, seemingly indicating witchcraft, but Hale quickly warns them that he is here to make such judgments and will not proceed unless they promise to believe his findings once he has garnered all the facts. While Hale, so far, has been described as wanting to do what is good and right, we see that he also fits into another category where Parris, too, resides, which is the category of authority that can never be questioned. This immediately serves as a warning to the audience that we are again in dangerous territory, since Hale is not necessarily the purely sensible man of reputation.

In the course of enumerating for Hale the various unusual events that the townspeople have no explanations for, Mrs. Putnam adds that she ordered her daughter to go to Tituba to conjure up the dead in an attempt to get some answers, which shocks Rebecca Nurse. Again we see dissension among the townspeople as Mrs. Putnam warns Nurse that, "I'll not have you judging me any more!" Hale listens intently and goes to his books for answers as all wait attentively, yet he provides no explanation of what he will do, but only repeats that his books have all the answers and that he will crush the devil if he is indeed among them. Rebecca is the only one to ask if the child might be hurt in the process. When Hale tells her it might be a brutal procedure, she says she must go and that she will go to God for Parris. He immediately questions her, fearfully and with resentment, "I hope you do not mean we go to Satan here!" The others, too, are resentful of her seeming superiority, again showing the disagreeableness in the town and pointing to the dividing line between the groups. Giles Corey is the only one left in the room from the Proctor/Nurse/Corey contingent. At this point, Miller interrupts the action in the written play to insert a description of Corey—a nuisance who is blamed for nearly every problem in the town yet who is innocent, independent, and very brave.

Hale turns to Betty, asking who has afflicted her, but when the girl remains limp, he turns, with narrowing eyes, to Abigail. As in the opening of the play, when Parris questioned Abigail alone, here again, new tidbits of information emerge. We learn that in the woods the girls danced around a kettle that a frog supposedly jumped into. The pressure increases on Abigail, with Hale reminding her that her cousin may be dying, and Abigail calls out Tituba's name, as if she is the only guilty party. Mrs. Putnam leaves to get Tituba, while Hale continues to pressure Abigail, to the point where when Tituba enters Abigail immediately proclaims that Tituba makes her drink blood.

When Tituba admits she has given Abigail chicken blood, Hale pounces on her with questions. Abigail interjects with more accusations against Tituba, saying the slave has made her laugh at prayers, corrupted her dreams, and tempted her. All in the room are against Tituba now, and when Tituba explains that Abigail asks her to conjure spirits and make charms, we realize that Tituba is telling the truth, since we know, although the others on stage do not, that earlier Betty revealed this as well.

The intensity rises as Parris says Tituba must confess or he will whip her to death. While we assume this is a metaphor rather than a literal promise, the punishment immediately intensifies, as Putnam cries that she must be hanged. Tituba is now terrified and weeping and suggests that someone else may be bewitching the children. With this new comment to latch on to, Hale and Parris squeeze Tituba for names of these others who are cavorting with the devil. The evil Putnam suggests the names of two women from the village. Hale explains that Tituba will be protected by God, who has made her an instrument for discovering the devil's agents. It seems that if she provides this information she may be safe.

First, Tituba, "in a fury," says the devil has repeatedly requested that she kill Parris, since he is a mean man, but she has turned down his demand, even though he has offered much temptation, because she does not hate Parris. Undoubtedly she believes this story may save her, yet when all it does is inspire gasps from those gathered, she proceeds to give them what they've requested—names of supposedly guilty community members. She says Sarah Good and Goody Osburn—the very two people Putnam had suggested before—belong to the devil. Mrs. Putnam reveals that Goody Osburn had delivered three of her children that died; now we understand why Putnam had chosen her name earlier.

Hale again tells Tituba that she will be blessed for any help she can provide, and with this Abigail cries out, staring and enraptured, "I want to open myself!" She now admits that she danced with the devil but wants to return to Jesus. She reiterates the two names Tituba has announced as being fellow conspirators with the devil and adds another. With this, Betty gets up from bed, staring, and rattles off two more guilty villagers' names. Parris and Hale are thrilled that Betty is back, but Betty still calls out another name, and so does Abigail, back and forth until a total of eleven people are accused. The only thing that seems to end their "ecstatic cries" of more names is the curtain falling to show the end of Act 1. It should be noted that many have postulated that in the nonfictional Salem of 1692 the repressive society drove the girls to dance in the woods, that personal vendettas caused some of the accusations, as well as the realization that once someone was jailed and condemned his property would be made available for sale to the other villagers.

Act 2 opens eight days later in the empty living room at the Proctor home, a sharply different setting than the previous crowded and chaotic Parris bedroom. Elizabeth is heard singing softly to her children upstairs, and Proctor enters from outside carrying a gun. The contrast between them is immediately set. Elizabeth suspiciously asks him why he is so late coming home, and fears he has been in Salem visiting Abigail. Proctor tells Elizabeth he wants to please her, rises and kisses her, but receives a lukewarm response and is disappointed. More of his sensitive side is displayed as he says they need flowers in the house, and when he looks out the door and poetically comments on the beauty of the lilacs.

Details of events outside the home begin to surface. Elizabeth says that Mary Warren is in Salem, which angers Proctor, since he forbade Mary to attend the trial, and since he sees it as a sign of his wife's weakness that she allowed Mary to go. But Elizabeth explains that Mary proudly announced that she must go, since she is now an official of the court. This is

the first Proctor's heard of a special court being
his wife explains that there are four judges in fr
well as the deputy governor of the province, who is in
Fourteen people are already in jail and could be hanged.
Proctor scoffs at the unlikeliness of this occurring, but his wife
quotes the deputy governor's promise to hang those who do
not confess. Abigail and other girls are greatly respected now,
and people are declared guilty based on if the girls "scream
and howl and fall to the floor" as if bewitched by the person
before them.

Proctor is "wide-eyed," and Elizabeth tells him he must go
to Salem and inform the court of his conversation with Abigail,
and her admission at her uncle's house that the strange
incidents had nothing to do with witchcraft. Proctor hesitates,
stating, "I am only wondering how I may prove what she told
me, Elizabeth," he explains. "If the girl's a saint now, I think it
is not easy to prove she's fraud, and the town gone so silly. She
told it to me in a room alone—I have no proof for it."
Elizabeth becomes increasingly suspicious of Proctor's having
an affair as he rationalizes his hesitancy to reveal Abigail.
Proctor's comment also brings to the forefront the tension
between the husband and wife. He is angry about her
suspicions and warns her not to judge him, saying he has been
so careful to please his wife ever since Abigail left seven months
ago. When he enters his house, he says, it is like entering a
court (a formidable comparison, since we know the newly set
up court in Salem is out of control). Yet even though he is
angry, Elizabeth, who he had earlier accused of being too weak
in dealing with Mary Warren, will not relent when she realizes
he has not been honest with her.

This stressful atmosphere is interrupted by Mary Warren,
who serves only to heighten the negativity and tension.
Immediately upon her entrance, Proctor confronts her for
going to Salem, which he has expressly forbidden. He rebukes
her for not getting her work done, especially since his wife has
not been completely well. Oddly, Mary gives a doll she has
made in court to Elizabeth as a present and remarks that "We
must all love each other now." She wants to go to bed, but

when Proctor asks her if it is true that fourteen women are now jailed, she lets them know that now there are thirty-nine. She starts sobbing and tells them that Goody Osburn is to be hanged but that Sarah Good will get off easier since she confessed to making a deal with the devil.

Mary says that in court Sarah Good tried to choke all the girls to death with her spirit and that, in fact, the woman tried to kill her many times before this. The Proctors keep questioning her, and Mary explains that she felt sorry for the old woman who is so poor that she sleeps in ditches. But then Mary provides a flimsy explanation of why she turned against the woman and why the judges condemned her as well. We find out also that Sarah Good smokes a pipe and that even though she is almost sixty, she is pregnant and husbandless, additional reasons for the upright Puritans to be against her.

Mary repeats that she is an official in court and will have to be gone daily, at which Proctor takes down his whip and Elizabeth tries to talk sense into the girl. Mary cowers from Proctor, and just as he raises the whip and reaches for her she points to Elizabeth, yelling, "I saved her life today!" With this, the whip drops and the couple finds out that Elizabeth's name had been mentioned in court but that Mary stood up for her and the judges dropped the inquiry. Mary says that by law she is not to reveal who brought up Elizabeth's name. This girl, who had earlier been described as quite mousy, now realizes she has power and turns to Proctor to make it clear to him, telling him that he now must treat her better and letting him know that she and the other girls just had dinner with the judges and deputy governor.

Once Mary goes to bed, Proctor and Elizabeth are left staring. "Oh, the noose, the noose is up!" Elizabeth says to her husband. She is trembling as they try to decide what to do, both believing she is only temporarily safe. Elizabeth asks her husband to go to Abigail and break her illusion, since it is clear that the girl believes that Proctor would marry her if Elizabeth were gone. There is great tension, and Proctor is angry and again disturbed that his wife sees him as deceitful, as if he promised Abigail something when they were together. "When will you know me, woman? Were I stone I would have cracked for shame this seven month!" he tells her.

As Proctor prepares to leave, Reverend Hale appears in the doorway, now more deferential, drawn, and perhaps feeling slightly guilty. The couple is shocked and frightened to see him as he is there out of his own concern, and not on official business. "I am a stranger here, as you know," he reminds them. "And in my ignorance I find it hard to draw a clear opinion of them that come accused before the court." This is a reversal in character from Act I, when he was completely confident that his books held all the answers. Hale tells them that he has just come from Rebecca Nurse's house because her name has been mentioned in court, even though he knows she will never be accused. This disturbs the couple further, since they know Rebecca is one of the most devout people in the village.

Hale explains that he would like to determine "the Christian character" of the Proctor house, and Proctor is immediately resentful but knows he must go along with the visitor. Hale asks why Proctor has been so infrequently at church and why his third child has not been baptized; Proctor explains that his poor opinion of Parris has dictated these actions, and this seems reasonable in light of what we saw of Parris in Act I. Hale still feels uncertain about these explanations, however, and asks if the couple know their commandments. Proctor proceeds to list them, but he cannot recall the commandment against committing adultery; his wife must remind him, causing more distress and pain for him to hear it pass through his wife's lips.

It is clear that Hale has misgivings about the Proctors, and Elizabeth, wanting to change his impression, asks her husband to tell Hale his information. Proctor, with trouble, tells Hale that Abigail said the excursion in the woods had nothing to do with witchcraft. Hale is shocked, and Proctor reminds him that many may confess to avoid hanging, not because it is the truth. Proctor explains as well his concern about going to court with this information, since the court has been so willing to convict good, upright people. Hale finally is impressed with Proctor, yet he brings up one more point, which is whether Proctor believes in witches at all. This time, though, Hale is disturbed by Elizabeth's answers, and her husband stands up for her.

Hale prepares to leave, but now Giles Corey is in the doorway and tells them his wife has been taken to jail. Directly behind him is Francis Nurse, whose wife has also been arrested. "They've surely gone wild now, Mr. Hale!" Elizabeth proclaims, and the others turn to Hale as well, desperate for help. Hale, while deeply troubled, has some understanding of these people but still has faith in the judges: "Believe me, Mr. Nurse, if Rebecca Nurse be tainted, then nothing's left to stop the whole green world from burning. Let you rest upon the justice of the court; the court will send her home, I know it." Ezekiel Cheever then appears in the door with a warrant for Elizabeth's arrest, and Proctor immediately turns to Hale, who had just told them there were no charges against her.

Cheever says he has been given warrants only just that night for sixteen more people, that Abigail has charged Elizabeth, and that he is to search their home for any poppets (rag dolls). Cheever says he does not want to search, and the Proctors say they have no such things, but he spies one on their mantel, the one that Mary had brought home that evening. Proctor says his wife will not go, and he sends her off to get Mary. Cheever examines the doll and is distressed when he finds a needle in it, explaining that at dinner that evening Abigail had screamed in pain and Parris had found a needle stuck two inches inside her belly. Abigail said Elizabeth's spirit had put it there. The clerk calls it "hard proof," and Hale seems in agreement.

When Mary appears, Proctor and Hale question her, and she admits she brought the poppet home and had put the needle in herself. Elizabeth is shocked to hear the story about Abigail, speaks out in horror against her, and Cheever takes note. Proctor grabs the warrant from his hand, rips it, and yells for Cheever and Hale to leave his house, calling Hale "a broken minister" for never once questioning the innocence of Abigail or Parris and for not recognizing that these accusations are prompted by vengeance.

After this outburst, Elizabeth says she will go, and Proctor is warned that there are nine men outside to help with the arrests.

Proctor again appeals to Hale that she should not be taken, and when Hale starts to reply that the courts are just, Proctor yells, "Pontius Pilate! God will not let you wash your hands of this!" Elizabeth is severely shaken, and Proctor promises to get her out of jail as soon as she leaves the house. When he hears clanking chains, he chases after the men, cursing them and yelling that they cannot chain her. Now Corey berates Hale, "And yet silent, minister? It is fraud, you know it is fraud! What keeps you, man?" Proctor is forced back inside by three men and screams after them that he will get revenge.

Hale advises the husbands that they must think of evidence that can be brought to court to counter the charges against their wives. Corey and Nurse depart, and Proctor tells Mary they must go to court together, so she can explain what happened with the doll and needle. Mary is more frightened and says she cannot do it. "She'll kill me for sayin' that!" she says and adds, "Abby'll charge lechery on you, Mr. Proctor!" He is shocked that Mary knows about this but stops advancing toward her only for a moment. Now, in addition to being angry he is confronted with his own hatred of himself. "Good. Then her saintliness is done with," he says. "We will slide together into our pit...." Proctor catches Mary as she repeats that she cannot go; he grabs her throat as if to strangle her and then throws her down. She sobs and continues calling out, "I cannot, I cannot...." as the curtain falls.

Arthur Miller added Act 2, Scene 2 to the play near the end of its run on Broadway. Many have said it is unnecessary both dramatically and thematically, and the play has been performed both with and without it and sometimes as **Act 3, Scene 1**. Laurence Olivier, while supposedly initially a fan of this insertion, later told Miller that while it expands the reader's perspective, in the performed play it destroys the underlying "marching tempo" and insistent "drumbeat." Some have said that the scene provides more information on Abigail, but, additionally, it tells more about her relationship with Proctor.

Proctor and Abigail meet in the woods, and Proctor is surprised that she is dismayed to be receiving so much negative attention. She tells him she is suffering from the pinholes on

rm and touches her stomach to show she is still
om Elizabeth's jabs there. Proctor sees her now
tells him that the town is full of evil hypocrites
and that she will speak out against many more villagers.
When Proctor asks her if there is anyone good, she says he
is—that he taught her goodness and removed her ignorance.
God has given her the strength to get rid of them, she tells
him, and she promises to make him a good wife when the
world is clean.

Proctor backs away from her and reminds her that his wife's
trial is tomorrow and that she has been in jail for thirty-six
days. He says he has come to tell Abigail what he plans to do in
court at the trial, so that she might think of some way to save
herself. But Proctor appears to have made a serious mistake.
Instead of destroying Abigail's hope of ever being his wife, he
goes to her and loses the advantage that he could have had in
court, possibly putting his wife at greater risk. He tells Abigail
he is giving her the opportunity to remove the charges against
his wife, and to therefore prevent him from having to bring
forth the damning evidence against Abigail and himself. Here
Proctor is concerned with his wife gaining freedom, not with
aiding any of his friends' wives or any of the others falsely
accused. Indeed, this shows him as less heroic than he appears
without the scene, and it addresses some critics' contentions
that he is too good.

Abigail acts shocked. She cannot believe that to explain her
vendetta against Elizabeth he will admit in court he had a
sexual relationship with Abigail. Abigail laughs madly,
trembling and looking at him as if he is mad. She says he is
hopeful his wife will die, and that she will save him from
himself in court the next day. Proctor is described as "amazed,
in terror."

We go to the vestry room of the Salem meeting house,
which is now used as the anteroom of the court. Depending
upon the production, this is either the start of **Act 3** or **Act 3,
Scene 2**. The room is empty, quite somber and "even
forbidding." Through the wall we hear Martha Corey being
accused of reading fortunes by Judge Hathorne. The stage

setting indicates that she, like the others accused, are convicted based on unseen evidence. They are interrupted when Giles Corey yells out that he has evidence, and we also hear the excited voices of the gathered townspeople. Danforth yells for order, and when Corey will not be quiet, he is ordered removed by Herrick and appears in the anteroom before us. Hale leaves the court to come to Corey, and Corey tells him he must make the judge listen to him. Instead, Judge Hathorne enters, yelling at Corey and calling him "daft," but he is followed by Deputy Governor Danforth and all become quiet.

Danforth tells Corey that he must submit his evidence in proper affidavit form and orders the attendants to take him away. Yet before any dismissal, Francis Nurse speaks up, and when Danforth tells him as well to write his plea, Nurse proclaims that the girls the judges have been relying on are frauds. This disturbs Danforth, who asks if the man realizes that he has sent four hundred people to jail so far and that seventy-two are to be hanged.

The talk is interrupted when John Proctor enters, guiding Mary Warren by the elbow, as if "she were near collapse." Parris becomes fearful at seeing her, especially when Proctor says she has information for the deputy governor. Parris speaks out against Proctor, but Hale tells Danforth he "thinks" they "must" listen to her. Danforth is very interested and hears that Mary Warren is there to say that she never saw any spirits. Concerned, Danforth asks Proctor if he has revealed this information to anyone in the town and if he realizes that in these trials the court has contended that God is speaking through the children. He questions Mary, and she says that the other girls are pretending too, that none of the townspeople have set evil spirits against them.

Ezekiel Cheever and Parris attempt to discredit Proctor. Then Danforth offers him a deal. He tells Proctor that Elizabeth claims to be pregnant, and if she is he will spare her life for at least a year. Considering this, Danforth asks him if he still wants to go through with presenting his evidence and being questioned, to which Proctor says he will, since his friends' wives are still accused. This shows some of Proctor's heroism, since part of his testimony will require revealing his own sexual sin.

Proctor will be heard in the court, and, surprisingly, even though Parris and Hathorne have been railing against Corey, Nurse, and Proctor, now Marshal Herrick unexpectedly stands up for Proctor. First Proctor presents a list of townspeople who've signed a paper declaring Rebecca, Martha, and Elizabeth to be good and to have never shown signs that they were in concert with the devil. Ninety-one people have signed, and Parris, now sweating, says they should be called to court for questioning and declares that these people are intent on attacking the court. Hathorne also pushes for the people to be brought in, while Nurse and Hale are against it. Danforth orders Cheever to bring the people in, making Nurse horrified and guilt-stricken, since he says he promised all of these people that they would not get into any trouble. Mary Warren suddenly starts to sob.

Next Proctor shows Danforth Corey's deposition, which looks like it has been prepared by a lawyer, but Corey explains that he did it himself, since he has often been unfairly accused and has had practice in court. He also tells Danforth that Danforth's father ruled in his favor many years earlier, which should be to Corey's benefit. Corey's deposition states that Thomas Putnam is manipulating the proceeding in order to gain land. Hathorne asks who gave Corey this information and the old man is shocked and says he cannot tell him, since this person will be thrown in jail as well. Hathorne declares that this is contempt of court. Proctor stands up for Corey, while Hathorne and Parris keep pushing for punishment. Finally Hale speaks up, reminding Danforth that the villagers now have an awful fear of the court. But Danforth retorts, "No uncorrupted man may fear this court, Mr. Hale! None!" This shows how out of touch Danforth is, as well as how consumed he is with having all obey him; it also shows a change taking hold of Hale, who not much earlier had also declared that the court should be trusted but now understands why the villagers fear doing so.

Danforth says Corey is under arrest for contempt of court. Corey lunges at Putnam, but Proctor holds him back, assuring him that their additional proof will sway the court. But Corey responds, "Say nothin' more, John. He's only playin' you! He means to hang us all!" This indicates the enormous power of the court not only to go forward with possibly killing the accused women but to destroy the men themselves as well and possibly others. Mary Warren bursts into sobs again, adding to the tension.

Proctor calms Mary and approaches Danforth to give him Mary's deposition, but Hale interrupts, saying that this testimony is so important that Proctor should have a lawyer. Hale pleads with Danforth, "Excellency, I have signed seventy-two death warrants; I am a minister of the Lord, and I dare not take a life without there be proof so immaculate no slightest qualm of conscience may doubt it." While Danforth listens to the pleas of Hale, he asks Hale twice if he questions Danforth's abilities to judge. Hale relents, and the proceedings that have seemed inevitable since early in Act 2 begin.

Danforth and the others read Mary's deposition, and Danforth seems quite stirred. For the first time, he berates Parris for interrupting once again, another sign that Danforth may be moving towards favoring Proctor's story. Danforth questions Mary as to whether she is lying or Proctor pressured her to do so, but Mary denies both points. The other girls are brought into court, and Danforth tells them Mary claims that she never saw spirits or any sign of the devil in court and that neither did the other girls. He asks Abigail if this is true, and when she denies it, Danforth warns them: "Children, a very augur bit will now be turned into your souls until your honesty is proved."

The questioning starts on the issue of poppets. Abigail says, "with a slight note of indignation," that Mary is lying when she states that Abigail saw her make the poppet (that was later found at the Proctor house) in court and put the needle in the doll. Abigail says that Elizabeth always had poppets, which Proctor denies, and both Hathorne and Parris chime in against him, finally pushing a furious Proctor to take another approach. He questions what Mary has to gain by making these statements.

Danforth asks Proctor if he realizes that he is accusing Abigail of a murder plot, which Proctor states he understands, to Danforth's incredulity. Proctor then reveals other points that he knows the judges will find disturbing—that Abigail was removed from their religious services twice because she was laughing and that she and the other girls danced in the woods naked. Ironically, the judges say that laughing during services is irrelevant, even though the religious character of numerous others has been examined in detail; the irony stands out particularly in light of Hale's questioning of the Proctors at their home. As for the dancing in the woods, this creates an uproar, even pushing Hale to finally speak up, and Danforth sees that the situation "is growing into a nightmare."

The disturbed Danforth allows Hathorne to question Mary, and he turns the examination to Mary's fainting and turning cold in court, which she now says was all pretense. Hathorne states that if this were indeed pretense then Mary should show them now how she did it. Parris chimes in as well, calling for a demonstration, but Mary looks at Proctor and says she cannot, and he becomes quietly alarmed yet still encourages her to try. Part of the feeling that Salem has gone mad is even supported by the way the court is run; seemingly it is a free-for-all, with Danford setting rules nearly at whim. Similarly, Danforth is not the only one doing the questioning; he has turned this over to Hathorne at this point, and even Parris is allowed to ask the girl questions. Additionally, the idea that those who confess to being witches will be let out of jail also makes no sense, since these people who were believed to cause great harm will now be free to do so.

The tension is sustained through this act by the jockeying for Danforth's favor, which seems to sway back and forth as the testimony wears on. After being pressured, Mary explains that in court she got wrapped up in the commotion when the other girls started screaming and when she saw how Danforth himself believed the girls. Danforth now seems to understand Mary and, worried, he looks to Abigail and asks her if this is what motivated her, too, rather than the presence of actual spirits. Abigail answers, "Why, this—this—is a base question,

sir," and throughout the rest of the act is see
and disbelieving that she should have to
questioning. She says that she cannot beli
mistrusted, and Danforth weakens. Also notew
calls Danforth the more common "Mr.," rather than "Your
Honor" or "Your Excellency" for example, as she boldly
threatens: "Let *you* beware, Mr. Danforth. Think you to be so
mighty that the power of Hell may not turn *your* wits? Beware
of it!"

Abigail, looking frightened and shivering, turns her gaze
upward and then looks at Mary as if she is responsible. The
other girls follow Abigail's lead; their teeth chatter and they
blame Mary for it. Mary emits a hysterical cry and starts to run
but is caught by Proctor, who then leaps to Abigail, grabs her
hair and pulls her up to stand. She screams, along with
Danforth and others in the room, as Proctor roars, "How do
you call Heaven! Whore! Whore!" Proctor is pried away from
her in agony, while Danforth is shocked. Trembling, Proctor
confesses in two short sentences that he committed adultery
with Abigail, and Danforth is now dumfounded.

Greatly ashamed and with a breaking voice, Proctor explains
that it happened about eight months ago, when Abigail worked
at the Proctor home. Miller describes Proctor as clamping his
jaw to keep from weeping as he continues. His wife dismissed
Abigail, Proctor says, nearly overcome and trying to gain
control. He turns away for a moment and then cries out about
Abigail, "She thinks to dance with me on my wife's grave! And
well she might, for I thought of her softly. God help me, I
lusted, and there *is* a promise in such sweat. But it is a whore's
vengeance, and you must see it; I set myself entirely in your
hands. I know you must see it now."

Proctor is noble enough to willingly accept blame for his
own actions. He uses nearly the same language his wife used
with him earlier in Act 2. She had advised him to understand
that a woman might see the act as meaning something more
than a man might, that the woman might believe the man will
change his life for her, even if this is not directly stated. By
using part of his wife's explanation, Proctor seems closer to her

and understanding of her position. While he repeatedly uses the word "whore" to describe Abigail, though, he never uses similar language to describe himself, one of a number of reasons some feminists are critical of the play.

Danforth is horrified, and when he turns to Abigail to ask if she denies all that has just been told, she remains contemptuous, saying she must not answer, and threatens to leave. "I'll not have such looks!" she proclaims to Danforth and must be stopped from walking out. Following another tactic, Danforth asks that Elizabeth Proctor be brought into the court. Again Danforth asks John Proctor to completely clarify that his wife fired Abigail because she knew her to be a "harlot." To Abigail, Danforth issues a warning. He has both Abigail and Proctor turn their backs, so they will not face Elizabeth when she is in the room.

Following this preparation, Elizabeth is brought in and looks around the room for her husband. Danforth warns her to look only at him and asks why she dismissed Abigail from working in the Proctor home. Elizabeth is hesitant, not knowing how to answer the question, since she wants to tell the truth but does not want to cause her husband trouble. She does admit, "I thought I saw my husband somewhat turning from me," but she will not go so far as to say anything else against him. She is in agony, since Danforth will not drop the questioning and finally holds her face so she must look only at him. He asks directly if her husband is a lecher, to which she finally, quietly responds that he is not. Her husband calls out to her to tell the truth, telling her that he has already admitted it to the court. Now Elizabeth knows she has unwittingly caused problems, but she is escorted out before she can explain.

Danforth accuses Proctor of lying and Hale once more tries to speak on his behalf, pleading for him to bring Elizabeth back into the court. The chances of Danforth changing his mind diminish, however, when Abigail screams that she sees a yellow bird in the rafters—allegedly the spirit of Mary Warren trying to attack her. Mary protests this accusation, but the girls in the courtroom begin to mimic her, as if under her spell. The atmosphere in the courtroom intensifies as mass hysteria takes control. Proctor tries to comfort Mary but turns on him, calling him, "the Devil's man!" Frantic, she claims that Proctor has hounded her and threatened her, quoting his supposed words: "'I'll murder you,' he says, 'if my wife hangs! We must go and overthrow the court,' he says!" She knows exactly the words to cause more horror, for all along Proctor and the others have been said to want to overthrow the court and make a mockery of its power, indicating how fragile the court and/or its supporters must be if there is constant fear of it being undermined.

Danforth turns against Proctor, who is dumbstruck with anger. Hale again attempts to implore Danforth, who immediately silences him. Danforth asks Proctor if he will confess. Proctor, wild and in disbelief over what has happened, says that God is dead. Parris calls out, reveling in the victory over this man, whose statement shows him, in Parris's eyes, to in fact not be an upright Christian. Proctor "laughs insanely" and then charges: "A fire, a fire is burning! I hear the boot of Lucifer, I see his filthy face! And it is my face, and yours, Danforth! For them that quail to bring men out of ignorance, as I have quailed, and as you quail now when you know in all your black hearts that this be fraud— God damns our kind especially, and we will burn, we will burn together!"

This pronouncement is striking for a number of reasons. First, even though Proctor realizes he and others are doomed, he speaks not of this but of his own guilt, showing how it has nearly destroyed him. He speaks of this even before he lashes out at Danforth, even though Danforth is grossly more guilty. Unusual as well is the fact that Proctor does not just condemn himself and then Danforth but that he puts them both in the same category. The hero has high standards for himself, and when he does not meet them he feels as low as the lowest. While some have criticized that Proctor is too good of a man, it seems we could also view his response here as a weakness, in that he sees his mistake as comparable to that of a man who is responsible for numerous condemnations and deaths.

Danforth calls for Proctor and Corey to be taken to jail. Proctor proclaims: "You are pulling Heaven down and raising up a whore!" Hale denounces the court and leaves, quitting his position. Danforth, who has hardly been open-minded with Hale, is now furious at losing him.

Act 4 opens that fall in a Salem jail cell. Herrick enters the cell shared by Tituba and Sarah Good. All around, the actions of the three show the strain and change that has taken place, even on these lesser characters. Tituba and Sarah Good speak in a mocking, almost delusional manner, as if they are indeed witches, and Herrick drinks liquor from a flask, giving Sarah some when she requests it. All are apparently worn from the last few months, as indicated by Herrick's remark to them that "it's the proper morning to fly into Hell."

Danforth, Hathorne and Cheever enter, and Danforth questions Herrick about the reappearance of Hale. Herrick explains that Hale has been speaking with those who are next to be hanged. Danforth is disturbed that Herrick has been drinking, and Danforth also comments, "There is a prodigious stench in this place," pushing us to assume that literally the jail is most unpleasant but that figuratively the whole place is in ruins. It is curious that Danforth himself makes the comment that can be read as a charge against his own self, although, of course, this is not his intention.

Before Herrick brings in Parris, there are hints of even further disarray as well as some revelations that are clear indications of additional problems. Something is going on in another town, Andover, but Danforth tells Hathorne not to speak of it. Also, Hathorne tells Danforth that Parris has had a mad look lately and that he has seen him weeping. Cheever explains that Parris is disturbed because of all the trouble in the village. He and other villagers are arguing now that many cows are wandering freely, since their masters are jailed and it is unclear who they will now belong to.

Parris enters, "gaunt, frightened, and sweating," and it is only now that we learn that Parris had called for Danforth. Danforth immediately berates Parris for allowing Hale into the jail, and Parris explains that it is actually a very beneficial occurrence, since Hale is trying to convince Rebecca Nurse and others to confess. Parris hesitates to tell Danforth something more that apparently is on his mind, but Danforth says he must. Parris says that Abigail has taken off, he is pretty sure, to board a ship with Mercy Lewis, and has robbed him of all his money. He explains that he believes they were motivated to protect themselves, having heard of what happened in Andover. Yet Danforth still wants to hear nothing of Andover, even though Parris explains that rumors are circulating in Salem that there has been a revolt in that town. Danforth is angry now, and denies this, yet Parris still tells him what the people in Salem have heard—that people in Andover overthrew the court and ended all talk of witchcraft. Parris warns that the same might happen in Salem.

Parris explains that since they are ready to hang the most upright citizens of Salem, the villagers have a notably different perspective of the court. Hathorne is greatly concerned and asks Parris if he has advice, to which Parris replies that they should postpone the hangings. Danforth immediately says this is not possible, but Parris explains further that now that Hale is speaking to the prisoners there may be a chance that at least one will confess, which should thereby force the villagers to accept that the court is right in its judgment of all imprisoned. Parris adds that only thirty people attended Proctor's excommunication.

But Danforth will not give in and tells Parris that he himself will go now and try to convince one of the prisoners to confess. Parris warns that he will not have enough time, since the group is scheduled to be executed at dawn. Still Danforth will not be swayed. Then Parris describes another frightening occurrence, saying that when he opened his door to leave his home a dagger fell. Now we understand why Parris has been so concerned about the hangings; he tells Danforth that he is in great danger, and we see him as unchanged in his self-centeredness.

Hale enters, exhausted and pained by sorrow. He immediately tells Danforth that he must pardon the prisoners. When Danforth remains unmoved, Hale asks for more time with the prisoners to convince them to confess. Yet Danforth is insistently against this, sticking to a weak explanation: "Twelve are already executed; the names of these seven are given out, and the village expects to see them die this morning. Postponement now speaks a floundering on my part; reprieve or pardon must cast doubt upon the guilt of them that died till now." Danforth rationalizes here in the name of being fair to all, not accepting that if there has been a mistake in the accusations that the moral man would stop the deaths now before many more are unfairly executed.

Danforth is prepared for a fight if the villagers provoke it, and he tries to calm Parris and Hale by stating, "If retaliation is your fear, know this—I should hang ten thousand that dared to rise against the law, and an ocean of salt tears could not melt the resolution of the statutes." Danforth decides he will take on convincing John Proctor to confess. In making the decision about who to attempt to persuade, it is curious that Danforth does not consider the testimony against the various prisoners but only if there is some hope of convincing the person, and if Hale had already made an attempt with the individual.

Danforth thinks it best to first have Elizabeth urge her husband to confess. While the group waits for Elizabeth to be brought before them, Hale tries again to change Danforth's mind. He tells him he will not be seen as weak but as merciful if he postpones the executions. But Hale does not understand that Danforth has no desire to be viewed as merciful. Hale also reminds Danforth that he may be responsible for causing a rebellion, and when he realizes he now has his attention he describes the chaotic state of the village, where orphans are wandering about, cattle are loose, and crops lie stinking and rotting in the fields. He warns Danforth, "[Y]ou wonder yet if rebellion's spoke? Better you should marvel how they do not burn your province!" Danforth asks him if he has preached in Andover recently, assuming that has riled Hale, but Hale says he hasn't. When Danforth says he cannot understand why, then, Hale has returned, Hale first answers sarcastically and then speaks of his own guilt. "There is blood on my head! Can you not see the blood on my head!!" It seems fitting that there are exclamation points after this second sentence rather than question marks, for there is no point in asking Danforth such a question; he refuses to see his own horrific mistakes and so could hardly see Hale's.

Elizabeth enters, looking poorly, and while Danforth starts to speak with her, he realizes his forte is cross-examination, and asks Hale to proceed instead. Hale explains to Elizabeth that he no longer is associated with the court and wishes Proctor's life could be spared; if it is not, he feels he is his murderer. Hale says that as a Christian he has struggled with the idea of trying to convince those who are jailed to confess and thereby lie. Hathorne denies that lying is involved, but Hale retorts that it would be lying since the people are innocent. Danforth says there can be no more such talk.

Hale begs Elizabeth to induce her husband to confess, telling her that there is no justification for taking a life, and that God may damn a liar who confesses less than he would a person, "that throws his life away for pride." But Elizabeth quietly states that this sounds like the devil's argument, a curious choice of words, since the men surrounding her are supposedly responsible for determining who is in allegiance with the devil and since John Proctor himself already accused Danforth of being the devil's advocate for accusing so many.

Since Hale is not making progress with Elizabeth, Danforth steps in, attempting to appeal purely to her emotional side. Yet he is surprised to see Elizabeth being unresponsive and unemotional. Just when he loses his patience with her, she says she will speak with her husband but will not promise that she will urge him to confess. John Proctor is brought to the cell, no longer appearing like himself but instead dirty and bearded. He stops in the doorway when he first sees his wife, and the emotional connection between them is so keenly apparent that the others are silent. Hale urges the men to leave the couple alone, which they do, but only after Danforth urges Proctor to confess.

The two are quiet as they look at each other in their dejected states, at the mercy of evil authority. Finally they touch and sit down, and Proctor first asks her about the baby she is carrying and about their other children. Elizabeth starts to weaken but stops herself, and he admits that he has been tortured and that his life will soon be over. He asks whether any of the others have confessed, and she says that a hundred or more have, but not those highly respected people such as Rebecca. He asks specifically about Giles Corey, and his wife relates the cruel, inhuman death he suffered. Corey would plead neither guilty—for he did not want to lie—nor not guilty in court, because if he pleaded not guilty they could hang him and auction his property; since Corey would not plead, his property would rightfully be left to his sons. But the court was not about to be outsmarted by Corey; they tortured him by placing large stones on his body, believing they could force him to plead. Still Corey would not give in, and so he died from being crushed.

Even after hearing about these instances of courage, Proctor tells his wife he has been thinking of confessing, but then he immediately asks her what she thinks of this decision. Elizabeth says she cannot judge him, and she says he must do what he thinks is right. She then says she wants him to live. Proctor explains his reason for confessing. He sees that it is the most upright people who are determined not to confess and says that he does not fit in this category; it is a pretense for him to be a part of this group, he says. God sees him for the man that he is already, and this confession will not change that perspective. He still asks his wife's opinion after giving this explanation.

Elizabeth warns him that her forgiveness means nothing if he cannot forgive himself. Now he is in agony over the decision, but she tells him that whatever choice he makes she knows that he is a good man. She then starts to admit her own sins, telling him that by being a cold wife she encouraged his cheating. He interrupts, not wanting her to take on any guilt, tut she continues. She says that he has had to take on her sins, and she reveals that all along she had such a low opinion of herself that she could not believe that anyone would love her; she lived constantly in suspicion, cold and unable to express her love to him.

Before Proctor can respond, the couple is interrupted by Hathorne, who asks what Proctor has decided, telling them that the sun is almost up and the deadline imminent. Elizabeth again tells her husband he must do what he wishes, and he turns from her to Hathorne and in a hollow voice tells him he wants his life. Hathorne asks him if this means he will confess, and Proctor repeats that he wants his life. This is a good enough answer for Hathorne, who runs off with joy, yelling down the hallway. Proctor and Elizabeth are left alone again for just a few moments, and Proctor says he knows Elizabeth would never confess. "You would not; if tongs of fire were singeing you you would not! It is evil. Good, then—it is evil, and I do it!"

Danforth enters with Parris, Hale, and Cheever, and Cheever prepares to take Proctor's statement. Proctor questions why it must be written and is told that the statement will be posted on the church door. Danforth starts questioning Proctor, who is not quick to answer, and Danforth tries to rush him by reminding him that the sun is lighting the sky and people are waiting at the scaffold. Proctor begins to answer Danforth's questions, and Rebecca Nurse is brought in, also seriously deteriorated, needing help to walk. She is happy to see Proctor but he turns away from her. Danforth tells Rebecca to take heed of Proctor's example, and as he starts to question him again, Rebecca realizes what is happening and calls out to Proctor, astonished. He stays facing the wall and, speaking through his teeth, continues to answer Danforth.

Danforth asks Rebecca if she will confess, and instead of answering him she again calls out, "Oh, John—God send his mercy on you!" Persisting, Danforth asks if she will confess, and she says she cannot since it is a lie. Danforth focuses again on Proctor, this time asking if he has seen Rebecca in the company of the devil. Proctor must be prompted again to answer, and quietly he says he has not. Danforth realizes he may not get the full confession he had envisioned, since each time he asks Proctor if he has seen a particular person with the devil, and Proctor answers that he has not. Danforth warns, "I am not empowered to trade your life for a lie. You have most certainly seen some person with the devil." Speaking of those soon to be hanged, Proctor responds: "They think to go like saints. I like not to spoil their names." Danforth is astonished and asks again who he saw with the devil, but Proctor will not give him a name.

Hale and Parris are fearful as they see the questioning turn sour. They urge Danforth to be satisfied with what Proctor has agreed to, and the deputy governor gives in and tells Cheever to give the statement to Proctor to sign. Proctor looks at it and says it is enough that they have witnessed his confession. But Danforth will not relent on this point. Proctor struggles now but then does sign the paper, and Parris calls out praise to God. But Proctor, apparently still in turmoil and now with a raging anger building inside him, takes the paper back as Danforth reaches for it. Proctor tells the men that they have seen him sign it and it does not need to be made public. He says that he will not allow them to use him and that it will blacken all of his jailed friends if his statement is nailed to the church door on the very day of their executions.

Danforth says he must have the written statement, to which Proctor replies that the court's word should be good enough without the paper. Suspicious now, Danforth asks him whether it is the same if he gives up the paper or not, and Proctor cries out that it is not the same. Danforth asks if he plans to deny the confession when he leaves, but Proctor replies that he will not and cries out: "Because it is my name! ... Because I lie and sign myself to lies! Because I am not worth the dust on the feet of them that hang!" With this, Danforth tells him that if the confession is a lie he cannot accept it. Proctor does not reply. Danforth asks him again if the paper is a lie. In response Proctor rips it and crumples it; his breast is heaving, and he weeps in rage.

Danforth calls for the marshal to take Proctor away, as both Parris and Hale yell to Proctor that he cannot destroy the confession. Full of tears, Proctor tells them, "I can. And there's your first marvel, that I can. You have made your magic now, for now I do think I see some shred of goodness in John Proctor. Not enough to weave a banner with, but white enough to keep it from such dogs." He is happy to not give the men what they want and now apparently is at peace with his decision. As his wife runs to him and cries, he advises, "Give them no tear! Tears pleasure them! Show honor now; show a stony heart and sink them with it!" He lifts Elizabeth and kisses her passionately, apparently now feeling free.

Rebecca yells that he has nothing to fear, while Danforth shouts for them all to be hanged. Rebecca stumbles, nearly collapsing as she is led away. We wonder if this struggle has been too much for her. Parris, still fearing the town will turn on him, begs Elizabeth to convince Proctor to confess. Drumrolls are heard outside. Hale, too, pleads for Elizabeth to talk sense into her husband, again arguing that Proctor's action is one of pride and that there will be no benefit from his death. Elizabeth, "supporting herself against collapse," cries, "He have his goodness now. God forbid I take it from him!" There is a final drumroll crash. Hale cries and prays frantically. The sunrise is shining on Elizabeth's face as the drums continue to rattle and the curtain falls.

Directly following the printed play, there are notes from Miller that reveal what happened to some of the actual people who appeared as characters in his play "not long after the fever died." Parris was voted out of his position and left town. Legend says that Abigail became a prostitute in Boston. Mary Proctor remarried four years after her husband's death.

Then twenty years after the last execution, the government gave money to victims who still lived and to the families of those that had been killed. Yet wickedness still surrounded the affair, since some money was given to those who had been informers at the trials as well. In March 1712 the congregation rescinded excommunications, following the orders of the government. Some farms of victims became ruined, with no one wanting to buy them for more than a century. "To all intents and purposes, the power of theocracy in Massachusetts was broken," Miller writes.

Critical Views

ARTHUR MILLER'S INTRODUCTION
TO HIS *COLLECTED PLAYS*

If the reception of *All My Sons* and *Death of a Salesman* had made the world a friendly place for me, events of the early fifties quickly turned that warmth into an illusion. It was not only the rise of "McCarthyism" that moved me, but something which seemed much more weird and mysterious. It was the fact that a political, objective, knowledgeable campaign from the far Right was capable of creating not only a terror, but a new subjective reality, a veritable mystique which was gradually assuming even a holy resonance. The wonder of it all struck me that so practical and picayune a cause, carried forward by such manifestly ridiculous men, should be capable of paralyzing thought itself, and worse, causing to billow up such persuasive clouds of "mysterious" feelings within people. It was as though the whole country had been born anew, without a memory even of certain elemental decencies which a year or two earlier no one would have imagined could be altered, let alone forgotten. Astounded, I watched men pass me by without a nod whom I had known rather well for years; and again, the astonishment was produced by my knowledge, which I could not give up, that the terror in these people was being knowingly planned and consciously engineered, and yet that all they knew was terror. That so interior and subjective an emotion could have been so manifestly created from without was a marvel to me. It underlies every word in *The Crucible*.

I wondered, at first, whether it must be that self-preservation and the need to hold on to opportunity, the thought of being exiled and "put out," was what the fear was feeding on, for there were people who had had only the remotest connections with the Left who were quite as terrified as those who had been closer. I knew of one man who had been summoned to the office of a network executive and, on explaining that he had had no Left connections at all, despite the then current attacks upon him, was told that this was precisely the trouble; "You have nothing to give them," he was told, meaning he had no confession to make, and so he was fired from his job and for more than a year could not recover the will to leave his house.

It seemed to me after a time that this, as well as other kinds of social compliance, is the result of the sense of guilt which individuals strive to conceal by complying. Generally it was a guilt, in this historic instance, resulting from their awareness that they were not as Rightist as people were supposed to be; that the tenor of public pronouncements was alien to them and that they must be somehow discoverable as enemies of the power overhead. There was a new religiosity in the air, not merely the kind expressed by the spurt in church construction and church attendance, but an official piety which my reading of American history could not reconcile with the free-wheeling iconoclasm of the country's past. I saw forming a kind of interior mechanism of confession and forgiveness of sins which until now had not been rightly categorized as sins. New sins were being created monthly. It was very odd how quickly these were accepted into the new orthodoxy, quite as though they had been there since the beginning of time. Above all, above all horrors, I saw accepted the notion that conscience was no longer a private matter but one of state administration. I saw men handing conscience to other men and thanking other men for the opportunity of doing so.

I wished for a way to write a play that would be sharp, that would lift out of the morass of subjectivism the squirming, single, defined process which would show that the sin of public terror is that it divests man of conscience, of himself. It was a theme not unrelated to those that had invested the previous plays. In *The Crucible*, however, there was an attempt to move beyond the discovery and unveiling of the hero's guilt, a guilt that kills the personality. I had grown increasingly conscious of this theme in my past work, and aware too that it was no longer enough for me to build a play, as it were, upon the revelation of guilt, and to rely solely upon a fate which exacts payment from the culpable man. Now guilt appeared to me no longer the bedrock beneath which the probe could not penetrate. I saw it now as a betrayer, as possibly the most real of our illusions, but nevertheless a quality of mind capable of being overthrown.

I had known of the Salem witch hunt for many years before "McCarthyism" had arrived, and it had always remained an inexplicable darkness to me. When I looked into it now, however, it was with the contemporary situation at my back, particularly the mystery of the handing over of conscience which seemed to me the central and informing fact of the time.

(...)

If *Salesman* was written in a mood of friendly partnership with the audience, *The Crucible* reminded me that we had not yet come to terms. The latter play has been produced more often than any of the others, and more successfully the more time elapses from the headline "McCarthyism" which it was supposed to be "about." I believe that on the night of its opening, a time when the gale from the Right was blowing at its fullest fury, it inspired a part of its audience with an unsettling fear and partisanship which deflected the sight of the real and inner theme, which, again, was the handing over of conscience to another, be it woman, the state, or a terror, and the realization that with conscience goes the person, the soul immortal, and the "name." That there was not one mention of this process in any review, favorable or not, was the measure of my sense of defeat, and the impulse to separate, openly and without concealment, the action of the next play, *A View from the Bridge*, from its generalized significance. The engaged narrator, in short, appeared.

STEPHEN FENDER ON PRECISION AND PSEUDO PRECISION

Writing almost four years after *The Crucible* was first performed, Arthur Miller seemed uncertain how to describe the ethics of the society he had tried to reproduce in the play. He notes, for example, that the Puritans' 'religious belief did nothing to temper [their] cruelty' but instead 'served to raise this swirling and ludicrous mysticism to a level of high moral debate'. 'It is no mean irony', Miller continues, 'that the theocratic persecution should seek out the most religious people for its victims.'[1]

On the other hand—and in the same essay—Miller claims that he chose Salem for the play's setting precisely because it provided people 'of higher self-awareness than the contemporary scene affords', so that by opposing the articulate John Proctor to an equally articulate society he could dramatize his theme of the danger of 'handing over of conscience to another' (pp. 44–5).

But Miller's audience did not always appear to understand the theme, and the play's reception was mixed. The author has his own idea of what went wrong:

> I believe that the very moral awareness of the play and its characters—which are historically correct—was repulsive to the audience. For a variety of reasons I think that the Anglo-Saxon audience cannot believe the reality of characters who live by principles and know very much about their own characters and situations, and who say what they know [pp. 44–5].

Most Miller scholars have more or less accepted his account of the play as the story of John Proctor at odds with a monolithic society. Arthur Hunt, for example, writes that the play 'comments on modern fragmentation by withdrawing to the vantage point, of a community which is whole and self aware'.[2] In an extremely interesting article on Miller. John Prudhoe interprets Proctor's stance against Salem as the 'most "modern" moment in *The Crucible*' because in it the hero works out his own solution 'unaided by comfortable slogans, the weight of opinion of those around him or a coherently worked-out philosophy'. Proctor's thought is free of the traditional beliefs of Salem and of the 'surprisingly articulate' speech in which the town expresses its values. Proctor's plea for his 'name' at the end of the play 'is the cry of a man who has rejected the world in which he lives and hence can no longer use the language of that world'.

This essay attempts to support Prudhoe's reading of *The Crucible* as a dramatic contest of language, but to question the assumption that he shares with Miller himself and with other critics of Miller that the Puritans in the play have a consistent moral outlook. Indeed, if one examines the language, both of real Puritans and of the characters in *The Crucible*, it becomes clear that it is the speech of a society totally without moral referents. Salem confronts Proctor not with a monolithic ethic (however misguided) but with the total absence of any ethic. The townspeople are certain of their moral standards only on the level of abstraction; on the level of the facts of human behaviour they share no criteria for judgement, and it is this lack which makes them victims—as well as protagonists—of the witch hunt. Their language reflects this complete disjunction between their theory and the facts of human action. Proctor finally demolishes their phoney language and painfully reconstructs a halting, but integral way of speaking in which words are once again related to their lexis. But the effect of this achievement is not to break away from the ethic of Salem; rather it is to construct the first consistent moral system in the play, a system in which fact and theory can at last coalesce. Proctor serves himself by recovering his 'name'; he serves Salem by giving it a viable language.

Notes

1. Introduction to *Collected Plays* (London, 1958), pp. 45–6. Subsequent references to this edition will appear in the text.

2. 'Realism and intelligence: some notes on Arthur Miller', *Encore*, 7 (1960), 15.

3. *English Studies*, 43 (1962), 430.

The fourth charge against the play, and the one brought by the more serious and insightful of the critics dealing with *The Crucible*, is at the same time the most challenging of the four. For Nathan, together with a host of other critics, attacks the basic structure of the play itself, claiming that it "draws up its big guns" too early in the play, and that by the end of the courtroom scene there is nowhere to go but down. This charge, indeed, gets at the very heart of the matter, and if it can be sustained it largely negates further argument regarding any relative merits that the play might exhibit. I submit, however, that the charge cannot be sustained—that, indeed, the critics adopting such an approach reveal a faulty knowledge of the play's structure and an inaccurate reading of its meaning. Indeed, Miller appears to me to have done a masterful job of sustaining a central action that by its very nature is "internal" and thus not conducive to easy dramatic development, and of sustaining this central action straight through to its logical conclusion at the end of the play.

The term "central action" is being used here in what I take to be its Aristotelian sense: one central objective that provides the play's plot structure with a beginning, a middle, and an end; when the objective is attained, the play is over. This central action may be described in the case of *The Crucible* as "to find John Proctor's soul," where the term "soul" is understood to mean Proctor's integrity, his sense of self-respect, what he himself variously calls his "honesty" and (finally) his "name." Proctor lost his soul, in this sense of the term, when he committed the crime of lechery with Abigail, and thus as the play opens there is wanted only a significant triggering incident to start Proctor actively on the search that will lead ultimately to his death. That this search for Proctor's soul will lead through the vagaries of a witch-hunt, a travesty of justice, and a clear choice between death and life without honor is simply the given circumstance of the play—no more germane to defining its central action than is the fact that Oedipus' search for the killer of Laius will lead through horror and incest to self-immolation. Thinking in these terms, then, it is possible to trace the development of this central action in a straightforward and rather elementary manner.

(...)

This structural significance of the prison scene may be observed in a careful reading of the play, but it is more readily apparent in a competent production. Thus, it is the business of the actor playing Proctor to convey to the audience the fact that signing the confession and then refusing to hand it over to Danforth is not, as has so often been charged, a delaying action and an anti-climactic complication on Miller's part, but rather a continuing and agonizing search on Proctor's part for his honesty—for the course of action that will be truest to his own honor and will recover for him his lost soul. In a dilemma for which there is no simple solution, Proctor first sees the efficacy of Hale's argument, that once life is gone there is no further or higher meaning. Feeling that his honesty has long since been compromised anyway, Proctor seriously feels a greater sense of dishonor is appearing to "go like a saint," as Rebecca and the others do, than in frankly facing up to his own dishonesty and saving his life. On the strength of this argument, he signs the confession. Yet, as Proctor stands there looking at his name on the paper (and here the way in which the actor works with this property becomes all-important), we have a visual, tangible stage metaphor for the struggle that is going on within him. Proctor, unable fully to express the significance of his own plight, cries out:

> Because it is my name! Because I cannot have another in my life! Because I lie and sign myself to lies! Because I am not worth the dust on the feet of them that hang! How may I live without my name? I have given you my soul; leave me my name!

The audience must see that this cry for his "name" is still the same search that has been at the heart of the entire play, and that here it has reached not some kind of anti-climax, but rather *the* climactic moment of the play.

(...)

Thus, a close structural view of *The Crucible* reveals that this fourth charge against it is also an unfair and inaccurate one. The play, however it may appear in the reading, does not, in performance, rise to a climax in the courtroom scene that cannot be equalled. Certainly the tension of the courtroom scene is great; certainly the prison scene, if poorly performed, could be a letdown. But in a competent performance the inevitable movement from the turning point toward a climax, technically called the "falling action" but certainly involving no falling interest or intensity, continues through the prison scene to that moment at which Proctor rips up his confession, after which a quick denouement brings us to a satisfactory, and at the same time stunning, conclusion.

DAVID M. BERGERON ON PARALLELS BETWEEN *THE CRUCIBLE* AND *THE SCARLET LETTER*

It is obvious in the presentation of the characters Proctor and Dimmesdale that Miller and Hawthorne share a common theme of the necessity of moral commitment. As with such plays as *All My Sons* and *Death of a Salesman*, Miller is in *The Crucible* again concerned with moral problems; and the moral vision of *The Crucible* is broader than that in the other plays, for here the individual is not the measure of all things. John Proctor must maintain his own integrity, and he must be morally committed to the community's welfare. He is, after all, part of the whole. Neither Proctor nor Dimmesdale can persist long in merely being spectators. The secret night on the scaffold must ultimately be transformed into the noonday brightness of complete commitment in the final scene of *The Scarlet Letter*. And Proctor must go to the court where, as Danforth says, "We burn a hot fire here; it melts down all concealment" (p. 85). He knows he will be stripped, but his moral obligation is greater than his selfish concerns.

(...)

One final theme links *The Scarlet Letter* and *The Crucible*, and that is the exploration of the human heart in which both writers uncover much dross among the gold. The heart may be in conflict with itself or with other people. Dimmesdale faces the problem of trying to be true to himself and to Hester, and the difficulty of it all produces anguish. He learns much about the evil recesses of the human spirit as he realizes his own hypocrisy and as he sees the evil workings of Chillingworth, of whom he says: "That old man's revenge has been blacker than my sin. He has violated, in cold blood, the sanctity of a human heart" (pp. 139–140)—which is for Hawthorne an unpardonable sin. Hester must give up her deception and inform Dimmesdale that Chillingworth was her Husband, and she says, "But a lie is never good, even though death threaten on the other side" (p. 139). Doubtless these words are still ringing in Dimmesdale's ears as he mounts the final scaffold. Might not Proctor have heard them too? Evil is a present reality in Hawthorne's fictional world, but good can be found, though being good, honest, truthful, does not carry any easy guarantee with it.

The Crucible contains also a probing of the human spirit, or perhaps to use a more contemporary term, the human psyche. Evil, vengeance, hysteria are all part of that psyche. The world of the play is, like Hawthorne's, filled with anxieties, frustrations, and pent-up emotions begging for some sort of release. When the opportunity comes, the outpouring is torrential. In short, the Puritan people, feeling always basically guilty, are looking for a scapegoat (or "witch" as they would say). Rebecca Nurse early sounds the warning: "There is prodigious danger in the seeking of loose spirits. I fear it, I fear it. Let us rather blame ourselves ..." (p. 25). But blaming ourselves is not nearly so comfortable as blaming someone else. Perhaps the Salem community needs the systematic and sophisticated way of scapegoat hunting suggested in Shirley Jackson's terrifying short story, "The Lottery."

Giles Corey ponders: "Wherefore is everybody suing everybody else? Think on it now, it's a deep thing, and dark as a pit" (p. 28). What is deep and dark is the human spirit which in spite of its virtuous trappings (namely religion) contains cesspools of hatred and vengeance. There are precious few in the play who recognize this and acknowledge it. Proctor and Hale do, but they are broken by the force of evil. Fortunately, there is also a residue of strength which allows them, especially Proctor, to realize that a lie is never good. This is the only way to gain any spiritual transcendence of the world. So the examples of Hester, Dimmesdale, Hale, and Proctor make clear.

If the visions of Hawthorne and Miller are not exactly alike, they are at least akin. And both share some similarity to yet another—Faulkner, who reminded us in his Nobel Prize speech that the problems of the human heart in conflict with itself "alone can make good writing because only that is worth writing about, worth the agony and sweat." They give us in novel and drama examples of man enduring and prevailing though torn by the world, and they doubtless could join Faulkner: "He [man] is immortal, not because he alone among creatures has an inexhaustible voice, but because he has a soul, a spirit capable of compassion and sacrifice and endurance." This is the affirmation of *The Scarlet Letter* and *The Crucible* despite the depressing realization of evil. For Hawthorne and Miller man must undergo the "crucible" experience by which some men are refined, but others consumed.

ROBERT A. MARTIN ON BACKGROUND AND SOURCES

The events that eventually found their way into *The Crucible* are largely contained in the massive two volume record of the

d in the Essex County Archives at Salem,
, where Miller went to do his research. Although
careful to point out in a prefatory note that *The*
t history in the academic sense, a study of the play
and its sources indicates that Miller did his research carefully
and well. He found in the records of the trials at Salem that
between June 10 and September 22, 1692, nineteen men and
women and two dogs were hanged for witchcraft, and one man
was pressed to death for standing mute.[5] Before the affair
ended, fifty-five people had confessed to being witches, and
another hundred and fifty were in jail awaiting trial.

(...)

Miller's addition in *The Crucible* of an adulterous relationship
between Abigail Williams and Proctor serves primarily as a
dramatically imperative motive for Abigail's later charges of
witchcraft against Elizabeth Proctor. Although it might appear
that Miller is rewriting history for his own dramatic purposes
by introducing a sexual relationship between Abigail and
Proctor, his invention of the affair is psychologically and
historically appropriate. As he makes clear in the prefatory note
preceding the play, "dramatic purposes have sometimes
required many characters to be fused into one; the number of
girls ... has been reduced; Abigail's age has been raised; ..."
Although Miller found that Abigail's refusal to testify against
Proctor was the single historical and dramatic "fact" he was
looking for, there are two additional considerations that make
adultery and Abigail's altered age plausible within the historical
context of the events.

The first is that Mary Warren, in the play and in history, was
simultaneously an accuser in court and a servant in Proctor's
household. If an adulterous affair was probable, it would more
likely have occurred between Mary Warren and Proctor than
between Abigail Williams and Proctor; but it could easily have
occurred. At the time, Mary Warren was a fairly mature young
woman who would have had the features Miller has
represented in Abigail: every emotional and sexual impulse, as

well as the opportunity to be involved with Proctor. Historically, it was Mary Warren who attempted to stop the proceedings as early as April 19 by stating during her examination in court that the afflicted girls "did but dissemble": "Afterwards she started up, and said I will speak and cried out, Oh! I am sorry for it, I am sorry for it, and wringed her hands, and fell a little while into a fit again and then came to speak, but immediately her teeth were set, and then she fell into a violent fit and cried out, oh Lord help me! Oh Good Lord save me!"[13] As in the play, the rest of the girls prevailed by immediately falling into fits and spontaneously accusing her of witchcraft. As her testimony of April 21 and later indicates, however, she soon returned to the side of her fellow accusers.

(...)

The second, additional consideration is that although Miller has raised Abigail's age from her actual eleven to seventeen, and has reduced the number of girls in the play to five only, such alterations for purposes of dramatic motivation and compression do not significantly affect the psychological or historical validity of the play. As the trial records clearly establish, individual and family hostilities played a large role in much of the damaging testimony given against those accused of witchcraft. Of the ten girls who were most directly involved in crying out against the witches, only three—Betty Parris (nine years old), Abigail Williams (eleven years), and Ann Putnam (twelve years)—were below the age of sexual maturity. The rest were considerably older: Mary Walcott and Elizabeth Booth were both sixteen; Elizabeth Hubbard was seventeen; Susanna Sheldon was eighteen; Mercy Lewis was nineteen; Sarah Churchill and Mary Warren (Proctor's servant) were twenty. In a time when marriage and motherhood were not uncommon at the age of fourteen, the hypothesis of repressed sexuality emerging disguised into the emotionally charged atmosphere of witchcraft and Calvinism does not seem unlikely; it seems, on the contrary, an inevitable supposition. And it may be worth pointing out in this context that Abigail Williams was not the only one of the girls who refused to include John Proctor in her accusations against his wife, Elizabeth. In her examination of April 21, Mary Warren testified that her mistress was a witch and that "her master had told her that he had been about sometimes to make away with himself because of his wife's quarreling with him...." A few lines later the entry reads: "but she would not own that she knew her master to be a witch or wizzard."[16]

Notes

5. For this and other information of an historical and factual nature, I am indebted to *What Happened in Salem?*, ed. David Levin (New York, 1960), hereafter cited as *Salem*; *Narratives of the Witchcraft Cases, 1648–1706*, ed. George Lincoln Burr (New York, 1914), hereafter cited as *Narratives*; and *Salem Witchcraft* by Charles W. Upham (Boston, 1867). I have also drawn upon material located in the Essex County Archives, particularly the Works Progress Administration transcript of *Salem Witchcraft, 1692* on file in the Essex County Court House at Salem. For a perspective of the events as social history, see Paul Boyer and Stephen Nissenbaum, *Salem Possessed: The Social Origins of Witchcraft* (Cambridge, Massachusetts, 1974).

13. Levin, *Salem*, pp. 52–53.

16. *Ibid.*, p. 56.

WILLIAM T. LISTON
ON JOHN PROCTOR'S PLAYING

John Proctor differs from all other characters in *The Crucible* in his linguistic habits, which are, as they are for everyone, a revelation of the real nature of the person. He uses metaphor to a much greater extent than anyone else in the play, and only he of those few people goes outside conventional Biblical metaphor to any great degree, though of course he derives some of his metaphors from that stock also. What this habit reveals is that he has a playful and imaginative mind, the same sort of thing dramatized in the seasoning incident which opens

Act II. This playful and imaginative bent is not greatly obvious, but it is there nevertheless, and it is the streak in his character which makes him a revolutionary, a threat to the community. It is worth noting that the word "imagination" never appears in the play (if it did, it would have a pejorative connotation, as it always has in the Bible), and that play, and images, are inherently sinful, as is dramatized in the poppet incident in Act II.

To put all this another way, John Proctor has the essential characteristics of a literary mind. He is capable of imagination and playfulness, and such people are always dangerous and disruptive. Plato would banish the poet from his republic because of his imaginative power to arouse our passions. The church forced Galileo to retract his revolutionary theory of the revolution of the heavens by merely exploiting his own imagination, as Jacob Bronowski points out: "He was to be shown the instruments of torture as if they were to be used." With Galileo's medical background, "His imagination could do the rest. That was the object of the trial, to show men of imagination that they were not immune from the process of primitive, animal fear that was irreversible" (pp. 214, 216).

Recently, Richard Ohmann has reminded us of the paradoxical nature of the literary profession:

> The literature we are to preserve includes works by Milton, Voltaire, Rousseau, Swift, Goethe, Byron, Blake, Shelley, Carlyle, Shaw, and others of that rebellious ilk. Beyond that, I think it is accurate to say that every good poem, play, or novel, properly read, is revolutionary, in that it strikes through well-grooved habits of seeing and understanding, thus modifying some part of consciousness. Though one force of literature is to affirm the value of tradition and the continuity of culture, another, equally powerful, is to criticize that which is customary and so attack complacency. That second side of literary culture is extremely valuable ..., since it ensures a difficult time for barbarism posing as humanity, for debasement of values, for vapid or devious rhetoric, for hypocrisy in all forms. (pp. 48, 49)

The passage does not seem immediately and exactly relevant to John Proctor and *The Crucible*, but it states in another way what John Proctor is talking about at the end of Act III when he asserts that he and Danforth are similar: himself the apparent revolutionary on the one hand, but with a great awareness of and adherence to the conservative tradition of which he is a part, and Danforth the reactionary on the other hand, who is gifted with intelligence and humor and imagination, but who refuses to give them the freedom necessary for their proper operation.

(...)

Broadly speaking, imagination, poetic and creative ability, and other such artistic characteristics are frequently thought to be essentially feminine rather than masculine, and largely because of their passionate and emotional nature, despite great historical evidence that these abilities exist also in men. And Abby, though never granted a metaphor, has great imaginative power, demonstrated by her ability to mesmerize the reasonable men of Massachusetts and break the will of Mary Warren when she claims to see the soul of Mary in a yellow bird up on the rafters. The physical attractiveness of Abby for John Proctor is obvious in the play, but, I think, so is the passionate imagination which finds its outlet in one way in her and in another in Proctor.

The distrust of the imagination and of imaginative literature, and of the people who write it and of those who are its protagonists, is a timeless problem. This distrust eventually closed the theaters in England in 1642, and in the recent past did the same in Greece; it prevented the establishment of a theater in colonial America.

DENNIS WELLAND
ON HISTORICAL ACCURACY

Miller provides a note on the historical accuracy of *The Crucible* which indicates the care he has taken over it, and reference to

Marion Starkey's account or to the primary sources w[...] substantiate this. (As many as possible of the or[...] documents bearing on the events and the trials were collate[...] a three-volume typescript in Essex County in 1938; that this was a Works Progress Administration project provides yet another instance of the influence—unexpected, belated, and indirect this time—of the Depression on Miller's work.)

Reference to one primary source, for example, *A Modest Inquiry into the Nature of Witchcraft*, written in 1697 by John Hale will demonstrate an obvious identity between Miller's character in *The Crucible* and the man who wrote at the time: 'I observed in the prosecution of these affairs, that there was in the Justices, Judges and others concerned, a conscientious endeavour to do the thing that was right'. Nevertheless, he is not easy in his own conscience, though what he questions is legal procedure rather than witchcraft itself: 'We may hence see ground to fear that there had been a great deal of innocent blood shed in the Christian World, by proceeding upon unsafe principles, in condemning persons for Malefick Witchcraft'. Hale is, however, still convinced that witchcraft may exist and that vigilance must be maintained: 'Seeing we have been too hard against supposed Malefick Witchcraft, let us take heed we do not on the contrary, become too favourable to divining Witchcraft [i.e. fortune telling]'.

The note of uncertainty, of suspended judgment, is very close to the keynote of *The Crucible*, which I find in the constant recurrence, on the lips of many different characters, of the phrase 'I think'. Much of the play could be summarised in Yeats's lines:

The best lack all conviction, while the worst
Are full of passionate intensity.

It is not so much a story of two ideologies in conflict as a story of conscientious endeavour in an uncertain world. This emerges with particular force and clarity in Act II, in, for example, such exchanges as this, in which Elizabeth Proctor tells her husband what she has heard from Mary Warren:

: Deputy Governor promise hanging
ιfess, John. The town's gone wild, I
of Abigail, and I thought she were a

...

ι, it is a black mischief.
think you must go to Salem, John. I
ust tell them it is a fraud. [pp. 53–54]

Joe Keller had asked in vain for guidance: no one could give it
to him. Willy Loman's bewilderment at Charley, who had told
his son what to do, is the bewilderment of the man who has
confidently inculcated in his own sons a complete set of values
that have turned out to be wrong (just as Ben's advice to Biff,
'Never fight fair with a stranger, boy', is, in its context,
implicitly criticised). In *The Crucible* the wiser characters do not
presume to dictate any one's duty to him, for that would be
asking him to hand over his conscience. Moreover, they
themselves are too perplexed by the conflicting implications of
the issues to be dogmatic. Elizabeth's quietly-delivered
suggestions here are the thoughts of a worried but honest mind
spoken aloud for her husband's benefit, and he replies in the
same key: 'I'll think on it ... I think it is not easy to prove she's a
fraud, and the town gone so silly'. Far from indicating a limited
vocabulary, either of character or author, the repetition of this
formula 'I think' is in fact a very skilfully-managed way of
suggesting the scruples, the misgivings, and the conscientious
earnestness which are all that these people can bring against
the diabolic impetus of the witch-hunt. It is significant that
Miller chose to dramatise the story of John Proctor, the plain
farmer, rather than the equally well-documented story of
George Burrough, the minister, who was also accused of
witchcraft and hanged for it. Miller's invention of Proctor's
earlier adultery with Abigail is not the outcome of a mercenary
desire to add a spice of sensationalism to the play. It is a similar
insistence on the human vulnerability of a man who is not a
saint, not even an ordained minister fortified by a theological
training, but just a decent man trying to understand and to

translate into action the dictates of his conscience, trying to do, not what he *feels*, but what he *thinks* is right.

(...)

In the theatre what comes across forcefully as the play's moral is the very Shavian one that in the life of a society evil is occasioned less by deliberate villainy than by the abnegation of personal responsibility. That is why Elizabeth quietly rejects as 'the Devil's argument' Hale's impassioned plea to her to help Proctor save himself: 'Life, woman, life is God's most precious gift; no principle, however glorious, may justify the taking of it'. Elizabeth, like Shaw's Joan, has learnt through suffering that 'God's most precious gift' is not life at any price, but the life of spiritual freedom and moral integrity. She replies to Hale in the play's idiom: 'I think that be the Devil's argument'. She believes this, but she cannot prove it: 'I cannot dispute with you, sir; I lack learning for it.' Again, as in *Saint Joan*, the learning of the scholars, the theologians, and the rulers is discredited, but not defeated, by the simple faith of a country woman.

WALTER J. MESERVE ON PROCTOR'S SENSE OF DIGNITY

Proctor, however, is the only character in the play with an ability to appreciate fully the silly side of people—more evidence of the fool he is to this serious society. He may well be the only one in the play who laughs and smiles in happiness and wonder. As soon as he has routed Mary Warren, at his appearance in Act One, he approaches Abigail with a "knowing smile": "What's this mischief here?" His teasing attitude continues and his smile widens: "Ah, you're wicked yet, aren't y'!" There is a light touch in their closeness, and she answers him honestly, explaining the girls' silliness. Then the mood changes. In the following scene among the adults, both Corey and Proctor exercise their wits to sharpen the edge of the growing confrontation with Parris. Corey notes Parris' expertise in arithmetic, while Proctor humorously compares his sermons to an auction, so much does he concentrate on deeds and mortgages. Proctor can make fun of Parris' assertion that there is a "faction and a party" in the church opposed to him, followers of Proctor. "What say you," he asks Corey with a smile, "let's find the party" and join it. He can also make fun of Corey and laugh not only at the old man's idiosyncracies, but also at his own expense in dealing with them.

(...)

As he tears and crumples his confession in the final scene of the play, Proctor makes a decision that is not easy to interpret with certainty. He says that he sees "some shred of goodness in John Proctor," and Elizabeth echoes this statement: "He have his goodness now." By such reasoning his choice reveals dignity and perhaps tragic stature, but there are other reasons of less than noble quality to consider. Proctor requires a sense of personal dignity, which he associates, symbolically, with his name; it is interesting that Abigail, in Act One, argues for her name in the same fashion. Proctor's sense of dignity, however is based not so much on what he believes, as on what he sees other people thinking of him. He is angry with Elizabeth that she judges him harshly and angry with himself that she has the evidence to think as she does. He will not trade his condemnation of Danforth's court for Elizabeth's life: "These are my friends," he says, "their wives are also accused—" This strong decision by Proctor shows both his "goodness" toward society as well as society's pressure. Later, rationalizing that he is no saint, he decides to lie in order to live, but he is cut to the quick when he must repeat his lie before Rebecca who has only pity for him. He can confess, but his back stiffens when he learns that others will see his name: he will not be used.

Essentially, Proctor can be false to himself and before God, but not before his neighbors. His choice, then, is made under pressure from a force outside himself in the manner of melodrama. Hale sees it in yet another way and describes it bluntly: "It is pride, it is vanity." In other words, Proctor is a fool to so waste his life when it is not necessary in such corrupt circumstances. Does he, therefore, choose to be a martyr and sin once more? Does he, like Willy Loman, choose a meaningless death for the wrong reasons? Or is he truly enlightened by a personal discovery? There is room for argument.

However it came, Proctor's decision had immediate consequences. It also bore the imprint, directly or indirectly, of all the forces in society that he had been contending against since he first discovered Abby: evil, superstition, gossip, vengeance, malice. This was the society, the people whose "moral size" attracted the dramatist. Anyone of several could have been the protagonist of a play. Elizabeth, saved from the gallows by a discovered pregnancy, would have been the heroine of a nineteenth-century melodrama. Rebecca's story is that of the staunch Christian martyr—a lesson in Christian dogma there. Corey, as a stubborn man, became the central figure in a melodrama by Mary Wilkins Freeman, *Giles Corey, Yeoman* (1893). Mary Warren is that guileless, lonely girl who knows what is right but can be led to her own destruction. Although it might be difficult to make either Parris or Danforth the hero of a play, both have the potential for character conflict.

James J. Martine on Tragedy

How would John Proctor fare, however, if he were to be appraised by Aristotelian measures? The play's action, first of all, is universal, applying to the lives of the entire community and not necessarily to one particular man. The historic events of 1692 and the 1950s make that fact eminently conspicuous. The plot of *The Crucible* is dramatic, complete, and unified. Its magnitude is grand (indeed, as shall be seen later, it is operatic) and is not only serious but has been faulted for being unrelievedly so. The play's hero is of generally high moral character and his downfall may be placed at the feet of his tragic flaw. Aristotle held that: "This error or frailty which constitutes the hero's tragic flaw consists in some moral defect inherent in the tragic hero's character which leads him, when the chips are down, to consciously and intentionally err in judgment and thereby commit some wrong act" (Stambusky, 93).

This deep-seated disposition or "frailty" is Proctor's own essential humanity and demonstrates him to be "a man like ourselves." And since this is so, the resultant catharsis arouses, and purges, our own pity and fear.

Does the play reveal a peripeteia? Proctor's reversal of circumstances has been too fully documented earlier to need elaboration or further comment here. And Proctor does exceed the limits of the then accepted social order, so much so, that, as has been seen, Parris and Danforth respond as they do, in part, because Proctor's challenge shakes the very social structure supporting the minister's and Deputy Governor's position and power.

As for an *anagnorisis*, that is a matter both simple and complex. John Proctor certainly and clearly achieves his profound recognition. Miller had especially chosen his ambience with this in mind. He has said, "In *The Crucible* I had taken a step, I felt, toward a more self-aware drama. The Puritan not only felt, but constantly referred his feelings to concepts, to codes and ideas of social and ethical importance" (*View*, vi–vii). This tragic self-awareness is the sine qua non to Proctor's situation and character. On the other hand, whether that *anagnorisis* can be said to apply to the unraveling or denouement of the dramatic plot to an audience is a thornier matter. One supposes that, as in all things, it depends upon the individual audience.

One of the principal Aristotelian tenets for tragedy would disqualify *The Crucible*: that character be held secondary to plot. As we have seen, Miller has not built his play in that fashion. Finally, there is the matter of language. Far from being stilted or awkward, as some critics contend, the language of *The Crucible* is elevated and poetic. Miller himself says, "I often write speeches in verse, and then break them down.... *The Crucible* was all written in verse, but I broke it up" (*Essays*,

277–78). In point of fact, one of the dangers in reading Miller's plays—as opposed to seeing them in production—is to find the dialogue and patois rudimentary or commonplace. Quite the contrary, the argot of Joe Keller or Willy Loman and the street-wise level of diction of Eddie Carbone, but especially the language of John Proctor, can at the same time be true to the demands of verisimilitude and qualify as poetic language.

On the other hand, to limit an appreciation of Miller's contemporary tragedy because it does not align with each of the Renaissance conceptions of tragedy or with all the dicta of Aristotle's *Poetics* is to ignore the uniqueness of historical period. Each age must, as Emerson says, write its own books: the rubrics of one age do not fit another. In its broadest definition, a tragedy depicts a series of important events in the life of a person; the diction is elevated, the play's progression is serious or dignified, and its resolution is catastrophic. It is a drama of lofty intent and deals, most often, with the darker side of life and human nature. All of this may be said to apply to *The Crucible*.

(...)

What does Miller expect of tragedy? Without question, he insists that the common man is as qualified a subject for tragedy in its highest sense as kings and princes. In his first and most famous essay on the topic, "Tragedy and the Common Man," he posits that "the tragic feeling is evoked in us when we are in the presence of a character who is ready to lay down his life, if need be, to secure one thing—his sense of personal dignity" (*Essays*, 4). Written 48 months before *The Crucible*, these lines apply to John Proctor as much as they might to Orestes, Hamlet, Medea, or Macbeth. Moreover, Miller explains that "tragedy, then, is the consequence of a man's total compulsion to evaluate himself justly.... The flaw, or crack in the character, is really nothing—and need be nothing—but his inherent unwillingness to remain passive in the face of what he conceives to be a challenge to his dignity, his image of his rightful status" (*Essays*, 4).

The Crucible is both an intense psychological drama and a play of epic proportions. Its cast is larger than that of almost any of Miller's plays until *The American Clock* (1980), because this is a drama about an entire community betrayed by a Dionysian surrender to the irrational; it is also, however, a play about the redemption of an individual and, through the individual, of a society. Some scenes, therefore, people the stage with characters, while others show the individual confronted by little more than his own conscience. That oscillation between the public and the private is a part of the rhythmic pattern of the play.

(...)

Today, compilers of program notes feel as great a need to explain the history of Senator McCarthy and the House Un-American Activities Committee as they do the events of seventeenth-century Salem. In fact, the play's success now owes little to the political and social context in which it was written. It stands, instead, as a study of the debilitating power of guilt, the seductions of power, the flawed nature of the individual and of the society to which the individual owes allegiance. It stands as testimony to the ease with which we betray those very values essential to our survival, but also the courage with which some men and women can challenge what seems to be a ruling orthodoxy.

In Salem, Massachusetts, there was to be a single text, a single language, a single reality. Authority invoked demons from whose grasp it offered to liberate its citizens if they would only surrender their consciences to others and acquiesce in the silencing of those who appeared to threaten order. But *The Crucible* is full of other texts. At great danger to themselves, men and women put their names to depositions, signed testimonials, wrote appeals. There was, it appeared, another language, less absolute, more compassionate. There were those who proposed a reality that differed from the one offered to them by the state, nor would these signatories deny themselves by denying their fellow citizens. There have been many more such since the 1690s, many more, too, since the 1950s, who have done no less. But *The Crucible* is not to be taken as merely a celebration of the resister, of the individual who refuses incorporation, for John Proctor had denied himself and others long before Tituba and a group of young girls ventured into the forest that fringed the village of Salem.

Like so many of Miller's other plays, it is a study of a man who wishes, above all, to believe that he has invested his life with meaning, but cannot do so if he betrays himself through betraying others. It is a study of a society that believes in its unique virtues and seeks to sustain that dream of perfection by denying all possibility of its imperfection. Evil can only be external, for theirs is a city on a hill. John Proctor's flaw is his failure, until the last moment, to distinguish guilt from responsibility; America's is to believe that it is at the same time both guilty and without flaw.

In 1991, at Salem, Arthur Miller unveiled the winning design for a monument to those who had died. It was dedicated the following year by the Nobel laureate Elie Wiesel. Three hundred years had passed. The final act, it seemed, has been concluded. However, not only do accused witches still die, in more than one country in the world, but groundless accusations are still granted credence, hysteria still claims its victims, persecution still masquerades as virtue and prejudice as piety. Nor has the need to resist coercive myths or to assert moral truths passed with such a final act of absolution. The witch-finder is ever vigilant, and who would not rather direct his attention to others than stand, in the heat of the day, and challenge his authority?

ERIC BENTLEY ON THE INNOCENCE
OF ARTHUR MILLER

"Great stones they lay upon his chest until he plead aye or nay. They say he give them but two words. 'More weight,' he says, and died." Mr. Miller's material is magnificent for narrative, poetry, drama. The fact that we sense its magnificence suggests that either he or his actors have in part realized it, yet our moments of emotion only make us the more aware of half-hours of indifference or dissatisfaction. For this is a story not quite told, a drama not quite realized. Pygmalion has labored hard at his statue and it has not come to life. There is a terrible inertness about the play. The individual characters, like the individual lines, lack fluidity and grace. There is an O'Neill-like striving after a poetry and an eloquence which the author does not achieve. "From Aeschylus to Arthur Miller," say the textbooks. The world has made this author important before he has made himself great; perhaps the reversal of the natural order of things weighs heavily upon him. It would be all too easy, script in hand, to point to weak spots. The inadequacy of particular lines, and characters, is of less interest, however, than the mentality from which they come. It is the mentality of the unreconstructed liberal.

(...)

To accuse Mr. Miller of communism would of course be to fall into the trap of over-simplification which he himself has set. For all I know he may hate the Soviet state with all the ardor of Eisenhower. What I am maintaining is that his view of life is dictated by assumptions which liberals have to unlearn and which many liberals have rather publicly unlearned. Chief among these assumptions is that of general innocence. In Hebrew mythology, innocence was lost at the very beginning of things; in liberal, especially American liberal, folklore, it has not been lost yet; Arthur Miller is the playwright of American liberal folklore. It is as if the merely negative, and legal, definition of innocence were extended to the rest of life: you are innocent until proved guilty, you are innocent if you "didn't do it." Writers have a sort of double innocence: not only can they create innocent characters, they can also write from the viewpoint of innocence—we can speak today not only of the "omniscient" author but of the "guiltless" one.

Such indeed is the viewpoint of the dramatist of indignation, like Miss Hellman or Mr. Miller. And it follows that their plays are melodrama—a conflict between the wholly guilty and the wholly innocent. For a long time liberals were afraid to criticize the mentality behind this melodrama because they feared association with the guilty ("harboring reactionary sympathies"). But, though a more enlightened view would enjoin association with the guilty in the admission of a common humanity, it does not ask us to underestimate the guilt or to refuse to see "who done it." The guilty men are as black with guilt as Mr. Miller says—what we must ask is whether the innocent are as white with innocence. The drama of indignation is melodramatic not so much because it paints its villains too black as because it paints its heroes too white. *Othello* is not a melodrama, because, though its villain is wholly evil, its hero is not wholly virtuous. *The Crucible* is a melodrama because, though the hero has weaknesses, he has no faults. His innocence is unreal because it is total. His author has equipped him with what we might call Super-innocence, for the crime he is accused of not only hasn't been committed by him, it isn't even a possibility: it is the fiction of traffic with the devil. It goes without saying that the hero has all the minor accoutrements of innocence too: he belongs to the right social class (yeoman farmer), does the right kind of work (manual), and, somewhat contrary to historical probability, has the right philosophy (a distinct leaning towards skeptical empiricism)....

Works by Arthur Miller

Situation Normal, 1944.

Focus, 1945.

All My Sons, 1947.

Death of a Salesman: Certain Private Conversations in Two Acts and a Requiem, 1949.

An Enemy of the People by Henrik Ibsen (adaptor), 1951.

The Crucible, 1953.

A View from the Bridge (with A Memory of Two Mondays): Two One-Act Plays, 1955.

Collected Plays, two volumes, 1957, 1981.

The Misfits, 1961.

Jane's Blanket, 1963.

After the Fall, 1964.

Incident at Vichy, 1965.

I Don't Need You Any More: Stories (as *The Misfits and Other Stories*), 1967, 1987.

The Price, 1968.

In Russia (with Inge Morath), 1969.

The Portable Arthur Miller, ed. Harold Clurman, 1971, ed. Christopher Bigsby, 1995.

The Creation of the World and Other Business, 1973.

In the Country (with Inge Morath), 1977.

The Theater Essays of Arthur Miller, ed. Robert A. Martin, 1978.

Chinese Encounter (with Inge Morath), 1979.

Eight Plays, 1981.

Playing for Time: A Screenplay, 1981.

The American Clock, 1982.

Elegy for a Lady, 1982.

Some Kind of Love Story, 1983.

Salesman *in Beijing*, 1984.

The Archbishop's Ceiling, 1984.

Two-Way Mirror: A Double Bill (*Elegy for a Lady* and *Some Kind of Love Story*), 1984.

Up from Paradise, 1984.

Playing for Time: A Full-Length Play, 1985.

Danger: Memory! (*I Can't Remember Anything* and *Clara*), 1986.

Timebends: A Life, 1987.

Conversations with Arthur Miller, ed. Matthew C. Roudane, 1987.

Plays: One, 1988.

Plays: Two, 1988.

The Archbishop's Ceiling; The American Clock, 1988.

The Golden Years and The Man Who Had All the Luck, 1989.

Early Plays, 1989.

On Censorship and Laughter, 1990.

Plays: Three, 1990.

Everybody Wins: A Screenplay, 1990.

The Last Yankee (one-scene version), 1991; (two-scene version), 1993.

The Ride Down Mount Morgan, 1991.

Homely Girl, A Life (with Louis Bourgeois), two volumes, 1992.

Arthur Miller in Conversation, ed. Steven R. Centola, 1993.

Broken Glass, 1994.

The Last Yankee; with A New Essay About Theatre Language; and Broken Glass, 1994.

Plays: Four, 1994.

Homely Girl, A Life and Other Stories, 1995.

The Theater Essays of Arthur Miller (revised and expanded), eds. Robert A. Martin and Steven R. Centola, 1996.

Mr. Peter's Connections, 1998.

Echoes Down the Corridor: Collected Essays, 1944–2000, 2000.

On Politics and the Art of Acting, 2001.

Resurrection Blues, 2002.

Annotated Bibliography

Bentley, Eric. "The Innocence of Arthur Miller." *What Is Theatre?*, 62–64. New York: Farrar, Straus and Giroux, 2000.

While Bentley says Miller's material is great, he points out many flaws in the play. He sees its villains as too black and its heroes as too white, specifically citing Proctor's innocence as unbelievable since he is accused of a crime not only that he is not guilty of but that doesn't exist. He categorizes Miller as "a dramatist of indignation," whose plays are reduced to melodrama.

Bigsby, Christopher. "Introduction." Miller, Arthur. *The Crucible*, vii–xxv. New York: Penguin Books, 1995.

Bigsby explains that the play's success now is derived not from its analogy to the McCarthy investigations but for its focus on the danger of guilt, the lust for power, and the natural imperfections of the individual and his society. It praises men and women with the bravery to confront "a ruling orthodoxy."

Budick, E. Miller. "History and Other Spectres in Arthur Miller's *The Crucible*." *Modern Drama* (1985): 535–52.

This essayist examines the evils of moral absolutism. While most assign this to the judges and other insecure characters in the play, this author puts Proctor in this category as well. He suggests that Proctor's trials are analogous to those of American Puritanism.

Ditsky, John. "Stone, Fire, and Light: Approaches to *The Crucible*." *North Dakota Quarterly* 46, no.2 (1978): 65–72.

Ditsky focuses on the play's popularity. He examines the play from a production standpoint, concentrating on the use of setting, language, and action.

Dukore, Bernard F. *"Death of a Salesman" and "The Crucible": Text and Performance.* Atlantic Highlands, NJ: Humanities Press International, 1989.

Dukore analyzes the dramatic structure of the play and shows it as organized around a central motif in each of the four acts. He also sees the play as divided into two parts, each with two acts.

Fender, Stephen. "Precision and Pseudo Precision in *The Crucible*." *Journal of American Studies* 1, no. 1 (April 1967): 87–98.

Fender argues that the Puritans only have an abstract perception of morality and this is what makes them victims and accusers during the witch hunts. He believes that Proctor gives Salem a viable language and consistent system that can combine facts of human behavior with moral theory.

Ferres, John H. "Still in the Present Tense: *The Crucible* Today." *University College Quarterly* 17 (May 1972): 8–18.

Ferres says the reasons for the play's continuous appeal is its concern with following one's conscience even when this demands going against the majority, and with reaching fulfillment by finding one's identity. He feels, though, that the play's message about heroism is mixed.

Martin, Robert A. "Arthur Miller's *The Crucible*: Background and Sources." *Modern Drama* XX, no. 3 (September 1977): 279–292.

Martin believes when the play opened it made audiences think of the McCarthy investigations but that now it's increasingly seen as a cultural and historical study. He describes the historical records Miller used to gain information about the Salem witch trials and other background, and he explains and supports changes Miller made to the facts.

Meserve, Walter J. "*The Crucible*: 'This Fool and I.'" *Arthur Miller: New Perspectives*, edited by Robert A. Martin, 127–138. Englewood-Cliffs, NJ: Prentice-Hall, Inc., 1982.

Meserve looks carefully at Proctor and to a lesser degree at Hale. He shows the thin line between the categories of fool and hero and describes John Proctor as having the strength and conviction to speak his mind but not always the best judgment.

Miller, Arthur. "Introduction." *Arthur Miller's Collected Plays*, 3–55. New York: Viking Press, 1957.

This essay was written a few years after the play was first produced and also after Miller himself was brought before the McCarthy investigators. In the essay Miller explains that prior to writing the play he was struck by the terror that the Far Right was causing as well as the new "subjective reality" it was creating. He says that this situation brought people's underlying sense of guilt to the surface, just as it did during the Salem witch trials. He counters critics who said his portrayal of the judges was too evil, saying there was "a sadism here that was breathtaking" and that he actually mitigated the evil in these characters but would not do so if he wrote the play today.

Moss, Leonard. "Four 'Social Plays.'" *Arthur Miller*. New York: Twayne, 1967.

Moss sees the play as focusing on the generation of hysteria and the gaining of moral honesty. He believes the play contains an implied optimistic conclusion but that it does not fit with the traumatic climax or the final sorrow.

Murray, Edward. "The Crucible." *Arthur Miller: Dramatist*, 52–75. New York: Frederick Ungar Publishing Co., 1967.

Murray argues against the critics who have proclaimed the play's characters are flat. He sees the main characters as developed and points to foreshadowings of their development as well. He agrees that minor characters are "flat and static" but sees this as appropriate.

Nathan, George Jean. *The Theatre in the Fifties*. New York: Alfred A. Knopf, 1953.

Nathan lays out four charges against the play that have been voiced by numerous critics: 1) the power of the play is all "internal" and not communicated to the audience, 2) it contains poor character development, 3) it is essentially propaganda and not timeless, 4) basic structure of the play is faulty, with the climax occurring too early.

Partridge, C. J. *The Crucible*. Oxford: Blackwell, 1971.

Here the play is examined in terms of whether it truly is tragedy, and in relation to the conflicts it reveals among men and women. Social and political background is provided as well as discussion questions, ideas for research projects, and a brief bibliography.

Warshow, Robert. "The Liberal Conscience in 'The Crucible.'" *Commentary* 15, no. 3 (March 1953): 265–271.

Warshow scathingly reviews the play. He says Miller has altered the facts of the Salem witch trials to fit his "constricted field of vision," and that Miller has nothing to say about these trials. He does not see the play as universal and believes the early audience saw it as showing the courage it took to stand up to the McCarthy investigators, even though he believes Miller makes no real statement about this situation either.

Weales, Gerald, ed. The Crucible: *Text and Criticism*. New York: Viking Press, 1971.

This text provides an extensive array of material, aside from the actual text of the play and other essentials such as a chronology and bibliography. Included are five pieces by Miller himself commenting about the play; as well as reviews of various productions; essays on the play and the playwright overall; primary sources providing background on the play's historical context as well as later contexts; as well as selections from other literary works that have themes similar to the play's, such as Shaw's *St. Joan* and Twain's *Tom Sawyer*.

Welland, Dennis. "*The Crucible*." *Miller the Playwright*, 54–66. London: Eyre Methuen Ltd., 1979, 1983.

Welland takes key issues critics have brought up and explains his own perspective: 1) the effectiveness of the analogy between the witch trials and the McCarthy investigations, 2) the historical accuracy of he play, 3) the play's concern with conscience, 4) Miller's use of language, 5) the love triangle.

Contributors

Harold Bloom is Sterling Professor of the Humanities at Yale University. He is the author of over 20 books, including *Shelley's Mythmaking* (1959), *The Visionary Company* (1961), *Blake's Apocalypse* (1963), *Yeats* (1970), *A Map of Misreading* (1975), *Kabbalah and Criticism* (1975), *Agon: Toward a Theory of Revisionism* (1982), *The American Religion* (1992), *The Western Canon* (1994), and *Omens of Millennium: The Gnosis of Angels, Dreams, and Resurrection* (1996). *The Anxiety of Influence* (1973) sets forth Professor Bloom's provocative theory of the literary relationships between the great writers and their predecessors. His most recent books include *Shakespeare: The Invention of the Human* (1998), a 1998 National Book Award finalist, *How to Read and Why* (2000), *Genius: A Mosaic of One Hundred Exemplary Creative Minds* (2002), and *Hamlet: Poem Unlimited* (2003). In 1999, Professor Bloom received the prestigious American Academy of Arts and Letters Gold Medal for Criticism, and in 2002 he received the Catalonia International Prize.

Pamela Loos has written and/or researched more than 35 books of literary criticism, covering authors ranging from Goethe to Cormac McCarthy. She is the project editor of *Women Memorists, Vol. II.*

Arguably the greatest American dramatist of the twentieth century, **Arthur Miller** is best known for also producing such classics as *Death of a Salesman* and *A View from the Bridge*. He has written screenplays for Hollywood as well as collections of essay.

Stephen Fender has taught at the University of Edinburgh. He has written *American Literature in Context, Volume I* and other titles and edited an edition of Thoreau's *Walden*.

Philip G. Hill has been head of the Department of Speech at Furman University. He has published *The Living Art: An Introduction to Theatre and Drama* and has edited several books on drama.

David M. Bergeron teaches English at the University of Kansas. He is an author as well as an editor or joint author of books on Shakespeare.

Robert A. Martin has been Professor of English in the Department of Humanities at the University of Michigan. He edited *The Theater Essays of Arthur Miller* as well as other titles.

William T. Liston teaches English at Ball State University. He is co-editor of *The Riverside Shakespeare*.

Dennis Welland, now deceased, was Professor of American Literature at the University of Manchester, where he also served as dean of the faculty of arts and in other administrative positions. He founded and edited for ten years the *Journal of American Studies*. He has written books as well as numerous essays on American and English literature.

Walter J. Meserve has been Professor of Theatre and Drama at Indiana University. He is the editor of many books, including *Studies in* Death of a Salesman and *Discussions of Modern American Drama*. He has been on the editorial board of *Modern Drama* for many years.

James J. Martine has been Professor of English at St. Bonaventure University. His books include *Critical Essays on Arthur Miller*, and the two-volume *Student Guide to American Literature*. Also, he is the editor of the three-volume *American Novelists, 1910–1945*.

Christopher Bigsby has been Professor of American Studies at the University of East Anglia, in Norwich, England. He is the editor of *The Cambridge Companion to Arthur Miller* and *Arthur*

Miller and Company. He is the author of numerous titles such as *Modern American Drama, 1945–2000* and has written plays for radio and television.

Eric Bentley is the Brander Matthews Professor of Dramatic Literature, Emeritus, at Columbia University. He has published numerous titles on theater, edited many works of dramatists, and also translated many titles.

Acknowledgments

"Introduction," from *Arthur Miller's Collected Plays* by Arthur Miller: 39–41, 47. © 1957 by Arthur Miller. Used by permission of Viking penquin, a division of Penquin Group (USA).

"Precision and Pseudo Precision in *The Crucible*" by Stephen Fender. From *Journal of American Studies* 1, no. 1 (April 1967): 87–88. © 1967 by Cambridge University Press. Reprinted with the permission of Cambridge University Press.

"*The Crucible*: A Structural View" by Philip G. Hill. From *Modern Drama* 10, no. 3 (December 1967): 314–15, 316, 317. © 1967 by A. C. Edwards. Reprinted by permission.

"Arthur Miller's *The Crucible* and Nathaniel Hawthorne: Some Parallels" by David M. Bergeron. From *English Journal* 58, no. 1 (January 1969): 53, 54–5. © 1969 by the National Council of Teachers of English. Reprinted by permission.

"Arthur Miller's *The Crucible*: Background and Sources" by Robert A. Martin. From *Modern Drama* XX, no. 3 (September 1977): 280, 282–83, 284. © 1977 by A. C. Edwards. Reprinted by permission.

"John Proctor's Playing in *The Crucible*" by William T. Liston. From *The Midwest Quarterly* XX, no. 4 (Summer 1979): 400–403. © 1979. Reprinted by permission of William T. Liston, Professor of English, Ball State University.

"*The Crucible*" by Dennis Welland. From *Miller the Playwright*: 56–58, 61. © 1979, 1983 by Dennis Welland. Reprinted by permission.

 Index

Characters in literary works are indexed by first name followed by the title of the work in parentheses.